YOUR LIFE, Interrupted

A step-by-step guide for writing

a home emergency plan that

covers your life's

big and little

interruptions.

Elizabeth M. Owen

2008

Trafford
PUBLISHING

Order this book online at www.trafford.com/07-1507
or email orders@trafford.com

Most Trafford titles are also available at major online book retailers.

Note for Librarians: A cataloguing record for this book is available from Library
and Archives Canada at www.collectionscanada.ca/amicus/index-e.html

Printed in Victoria, BC, Canada.

ISBN: 978-1-4251-3792-2 (soft)
ISBN: 978-1-4251-3793-9 (ebook)

*We at Trafford believe that it is the responsibility of us all, as both individuals
and corporations, to make choices that are environmentally and socially sound.
You, in turn, are supporting this responsible conduct each time you purchase a
Trafford book, or make use of our publishing services. To find out how you are
helping, please visit www.trafford.com/responsiblepublishing.html*

*Our mission is to efficiently provide the world's finest, most comprehensive
book publishing service, enabling every author to experience success.
To find out how to publish your book, your way, and have it available
worldwide, visit us online at www.trafford.com/10510*

Trafford rev. 7/2/2009

www.trafford.com

North America & international
toll-free: 1 888 232 4444 (USA & Canada)
phone: 250 383 6864 ♦ fax: 250 383 6804 ♦ email: info@trafford.com

Dedication

I dedicate this book to my parents, Ann and Harry. I really appreciate the love, guidance, and support you have given throughout my life and all my adventures. I couldn't have asked for any better!

Special Thanks

I could not have gotten this far with this book without the help and support of others. Although there are many who have encouraged me, I would like to especially recognize: my siblings (Bill, Marie, and Judy) who always provide a cheering section; Sister Helen McGuire for pushing me to complete my education; Barbara Herrin for the many free hours of support, editing, and input; the many teachers who contributed to my education from both Regis University (Denver, CO) and Southern Polytechnic State University (Marietta, GA); and everyone else who provided me with encouragement during this process.

Elizabeth M. Owen

Contents

Introduction

Elizabeth M. Owen

H istory shows that those who prepare for life-disrupting events do much better than those who do not. Take the story of Noah, for instance. It was a great idea to build the ark before the rains came. All the creatures who marched onto the ark not only survived the flood but, as the story goes, were able to continue their species. Or maybe you remember the emergency landing of United Airlines flight 232 in Sioux City in 1989? As the stricken plane somersaulted down the runway in a fireball, the crew used their often-practiced emergency procedures to help reduce the loss of life. Their training, coupled with the fact response teams on the ground had practiced rescuing passengers from a crashed jumbo jet, contributed to the survival of 184 passengers. Then there are the founding fathers. They designed the US Constitution so that if a serving president died in office, for whatever reason, a pre-determined line of succession would allow for an orderly transfer of power, as happened when John F Kennedy was assassinated. The average American's life would continue as before, with little or no disruption.

On the flip side, most of us can recall disasters where there was no planning, or the planning was so inadequate it resulted in massive losses. The Titanic sailed without enough life boats to accommodate all the passengers and crew, and thousands died as a result. One fire in July 1871 in Chicago burned for three days, killing 250,000 people and destroying upwards of 17,000 buildings valued at more than $192 million (goodness knows what that would be worth today). This event was blamed mostly on the rapid expansion of the city, and the planners' consequent disregard for safety issues. More recently, there was no warning system in place prior to the tsunami off the coast of Indonesia in December 2004 that killed 226,000 people and devastated 12 countries. And I don't think we will ever forget Hurricane Katrina, which embodied the concept of being unprepared.

These are all examples of major catastrophes, but what if the disaster hit closer to home, and was focused on your family? What if your spouse died unexpectedly? What if there was a gas leak in your neighborhood and you had to evacuate your home immediately? How about losing supply from a utility for more than a few hours (like the blackout of 2003 in the northeast)? What if your office burned down tomorrow and you lost your job because your employer had no recovery plan? Any one of these events would definitely interrupt your life to some degree. So what would you do first? Is there anything you *need* to do first? What's your recovery plan? And what if *you* didn't make it? Would other family members know what to do?

If you already had an emergency plan, you would know the answers to these questions. That's what this book is all about.

I am here to tell you anyone who wants to write an emergency plan (and that should be everyone) can. It's not rocket science. You don't need to have previous experience writing disaster plans or hold a degree in homeland security to be successful. What you do need is to understand two things: first, preparing a plan *before* any event occurs gives you the best chance of survival and recovery. Second, it's important for *you* to take control of *your* planning process rather than outsourcing it by hoping the government will step in and take care of you in the event of an emergency.

By following the step-by-step instructions in this book, you too can write a common sense, Budget-wise options, Time-wise options, tested, and easily-maintained emergency plan.

My hope is that, using this book as a guide, you will actually follow the steps outlined and write an emergency plan. I guarantee the mere fact that you have a written plan gives you – and each of your loved ones – a much better chance of being prepared for, surviving, and recovering from any life-interrupting event.

1

Overview

A year from now you may wish you had started today.
KAREN LAMB

Hurricane, fatal car crash, robbery, identity theft, terrorist attack, flood, quarantine, landslide, disease epidemic, house fire...

I could go on and on listing different types of disasters, each with their own magnitude of destruction and negative impact on your life. The truth is, disasters can happen to anyone, anywhere at anytime, and the key to survival is being prepared *before* it happens.

So, what are you doing to get your family or household ready?

My guess is, so far you have done virtually nothing. If this is the case, you're not alone. In a 2007 survey, the American Red Cross found that "the majority of Americans remain unprepared....and 23% have not taken a single action."

If you feel you are part of this American majority, you've come to the right place.

What is an emergency plan?

An emergency plan is:

- A written set of steps to follow should a disaster strike
- Written before it is needed
- Tested before it is needed
- Maintained year-after-year as changes occur in your home

Who needs an emergency plan?

Quite simply, everyone needs an emergency plan – singles, married couples, partners, housemates or room mates, families with children, multi-generational households, homes with pets, millionaires, single parents, renters, those living from paycheck to paycheck, and mortgage holders.

No matter your specific family or household configuration, you need an emergency plan for your home.

Reasons for not planning

People give many reasons for not having a plan. Here are a few of the most common ones:

I don't know how to write one. This is a legitimate reason – until now. In the course of my research, I found no publication that provided step-by-step instructions for creating a comprehensive, customized, emergency plan that covers preparation, survival, and recovery. Now, with the publication of this book, *this* excuse is off the table.

I don't have time. If you write the plan now, *before* you need it, you can think through the process calmly, test it, and amend it if you find something does not work as anticipated.

Or you can wait, and begin your planning when you are in the middle of your disaster. You will be forced to generate your plan on the fly, with nothing prepared, and you may have little or no time to collect the resources needed to make your recovery happen.

I'll leave you to decide which time is most convenient and effective for you.

It won't happen to me. Maybe it will and maybe it won't. I can't predict the future, and neither can you. But, if you don't prepare, your family are the ones that will suffer the most as a result of you avoiding this responsibility, should something happen. If you do prepare, your family will reap the benefits of your efforts.

I have a Will and life insurance. While a Will does address your assets and their disbursement after your death, often it is not read until 30-90 days *after* someone has died. By then, no matter what your Will said, it may be too late.

Life insurance can help compensate your survivors in the event of your death, but do they know where your policies are, and who to contact to claim on them? And when was the last time you reviewed these policies to make sure your coverage is adequate for your family today? Worst case is when your disaster is not covered by your insurance, in which case the insurance is not worth the paper it's written on.

I don't have the money (or don't want to spend my money on this stuff). If you are in a situation where it is difficult to make it from paycheck to paycheck, you might not be able to purchase water, food, medical supplies, etc. and put them aside just in case a disaster happens. Others may have the money, but just don't want to spend it on a kit, or some of the other stuff that is recommended. I understand. In this book, you'll learn that an emergency plan can – and should – be done on *any* budget, because it provides alternative ways to address each requirement, many of which require little or no cash.

I don't want to talk about the topic – it's unpleasant. Think about it this way. The events that create a need to write a plan *are* unpleasant – hurricanes, tornados, losing a job, house fires, death, terrorism, etc. But, your plan is not about these unpleasant topics. Instead, your written plan is an organized, prepared *plan of action* you can follow if confronted by a disaster. Writing a plan increases *your* family's odds of successfully surviving and recovering from anything thrown their way – no matter how brutal or unanticipated the event. This is not so much about death and destruction as it is about survival and recovery, and how your family can position itself to be more likely to survive the disaster and then get its life back on track.

At this point, I'm afraid you are left with only one excuse for not preparing an emergency plan: it is not high enough on your list of priorities.

All I can say is, it's your family – your choice.

What is the cost of failing to plan?

Best case scenario, without a written plan, you are confident you can find the time, resources, finances, and resolve to recover *after* an event occurs.

On the other hand, at worst, failing to plan may result in the loss of lives, total destruction of property, and/or financial ruin for you and your loved ones.

You choose.

New approach

I really want you to write an emergency plan, so I am introducing a new approach to writing such a plan. I am going to deviate from the oft-used methodologies for emergency planning supported by the American Red Cross and Homeland Security in two ways.

First, instead of focusing on every *possible* event that *might* happen, *YOUR LIFE, Interrupted* focuses on the one potential *result* that can arise out of any disaster – loss. Whether you lose your spouse as the result of a heart attack, a car crash or a terrorist attack, the impact is the same – your spouse is gone. In *YOUR LIFE, Interrupted,* you address the loss of an adult family member only once, and show how the steps that are required to continue without this person can be applied in any situation.

Second, instead of just preparing to survive for the first 72 hours following an event, *YOUR LIFE, Interrupted* shows you how to continue beyond that point, and includes steps for recovery. After all, once you survive any type of event, you need to put your life back together. Think about the survivors of Hurricane Katrina. Having survived the Hurricane, the hardest part of the struggle was still ahead of them – how to get back to normal. To do this, you must prepare for recovery *before* any disaster strikes.

Why you need to write your plan

There are four reasons you need to *write* your plan. These are:

- If the entire plan is not written but, instead, held in someone's head, then that person *must* be present at, and survive, *all* disasters. This assumes that the entire household is together all of the time, which is unrealistic.

- When grief overwhelms some or all immediate family members, a written plan can be handed off to a friend or relative to begin the initial steps towards recovery, such as notifying other family members, friends, places of work/school, etc. Those who need to grieve can do so, while others keep necessary activities on track.

- If the author of the plan does not survive, other family members can pick up the plan and move forward if it is written. This could be the last and most important thing the author of the plan does for his/her family.

- A written plan reduces the time needed to test and maintain your plan year after year.

Steps in writing a plan

I have grouped the steps needed to write an emergency plan into four phases. These are:

- **Phase 1 – Know What Can Happen.** You need to understand that the risks you face each day consist of much more than just terrorist attacks and natural disasters. Given the community and area in which you live, certain disasters will be more likely to occur than others. Knowing what these are, their warning signals, and how you can minimize your loss, is critical to preparation, survival and recovery.

- **Phase 2 – Writing Your Plan.** Here, you write down the steps your family should take in response to 14 different loss scenarios. I call each of these action plans. You basically lay out the steps to take if you lost your home, your job, a family member, a pet, etc. This includes identifying the resources needed to accomplish each step of each action plan.

- **Phase 3 – Collecting Resources.** You can now proceed to assemble the resources identified in Phase 2. These can include specific information, kits, documents, etc., so they are on hand if/when they are needed.

- **Phase 4 – Maintenance and Testing.** This is where the rubber meets the road. You make sure your plan works, before you need to use it. And, spending a couple of hours each month maintaining the plan ensures that it's up to date and always ready for use.

Writing format

You can use whatever is at your disposal to write your plan. If you have access to a computer and word processing software, you can use this to record and update your plan. If you only have paper and a pen, then write your plan by hand. I have provided examples of form layouts throughout this book, but it's important to remember that this is *your* plan, and you should design it in whatever format works best for you. Bottom line though, it absolutely must be written down, so others can access it and use it at any time, under any circumstances.

One recommendation

Knowledge is power. I highly recommend you include all family or household members in writing and designing your plan where possible. The more everyone is involved in the process, and the more they know, the better their chances for survival and recovery – whether you are there or not. Don't forget to include children, and make sure that family members who live in other areas know about your plan, just in case.

Disclaimer

This book is designed to provide general guidelines and directions on how to write an emergency plan. It is given with the understanding it does **_not_** provide legal, accounting, or other professional services. I have noted where you may want to seek the services of an expert.

No two plans will be identical. You and your family should customize your own plan using the guidelines and directions provided.

YOUR LIFE, Interrupted is designed to supplement all the free information that is available from several organizations and companies, including Red Cross and Homeland Security, by giving structure and directions.

Every effort has been made to make this book as accurate and complete as possible, however it has been written as a general guide, based on information available at the time of publication.

With this overview in mind, you should begin writing your emergency plan immediately. I have written my own emergency plan using the process and forms presented in *YOUR LIFE, Interrupted*, and each and every step has been thoroughly tested. Now it's your turn.

PHASE 1

Know What Can Happen

Elizabeth M. Owen

Yes, I did say this book focuses on what you can *lose*, rather than on every *possible* disaster that *might* happen, but I'm going to start by listing 46 disastrous events, just so you can understand that you are at risk from much more than just terrorism and natural occurrences. And, depending on where you live, how you prepare to survive and recover from a disaster depends largely on what can conceivably happen to you.

For example, if you live in a small town, you're probably less likely to experience a terrorist attack than someone living in Los Angeles or New York, but don't kid yourself. You still face the possibility of any number of events which can produce the same impacts (death of a family member, property destruction, inability to communicate with loved ones, loss of jobs, chemical release from a factory, etc.).

Another reason to know what can happen has to do with warning signals. Does your community use any kind of warning signals to alert you to an impending disaster? Do you know what they are, and what they mean? What about your children and/or visitors? Would they know what to do if they heard or saw one of these warning signals?

Based on where you live, and the natural disasters you potentially face, should you place Grandma's expensive antique dresser upstairs or downstairs so that it is less likely to be destroyed in the event of a disaster?

Is 72 hours really long enough to be prepared to survive without help from first responders or, based on where you live, should you make that longer (or shorter)?

Are there any risks around your home you have not even thought about as posing a hazard? For example, how close do deadly chemicals come to your home when they are being transported in trucks on a highway or in a railroad car? If there were an accident, could you be at risk?

How prepared are your local and state authorities to handle any of the events you have identified may occur where you live?

Although the focus of this book is on loss, you need to have a good understanding of what can cause this loss to properly evaluate your potential for loss. As you prepare your plan, keep this in mind.

2

List of Events

An investment in knowledge pays the best interest.
BENJAMIN FRANKLIN

There are four reasons I suggest you start out creating your emergency plan by really understanding what poses risks for you and your household.

- First, you need to understand your family is at risk from more than just natural disasters and terrorist attacks.

- Second, many of the risks you face come with some type of warning. The most common is your home smoke alarm. You need to identify which risks provide some kind of warning, be familiar with the warning, know how much time you have to get to safety, and know what it means to get safe. Since warning systems vary from community to community, the first time you or any member of your family receive a warning should not be during a real disaster. That's too late.

- Third, knowing what poses a risk to your family helps you face your potential for losses. If you think it cannot happen to you, this exercise may just open your eyes and change your thinking about the need to prepare an emergency plan.

- Fourth, once your plan is completely written and tested, you move into a maintenance phase. In this stage, you begin focusing your emergency planning efforts on educating other family members. If you know what events are most likely to affect the area where you live, you can focus your educational efforts on those events.

List of 46

I have compiled a list of 46 events which may or may not have the potential to be present in your life. I recommend that in the first instance, you quickly review the entire list. Then, you should:

1. Read the description. Be sure to not only consider your residence, family members or pets, but to also consider any major factories, businesses, and transportation infrastructure near your home. For example, most likely you will not receive a bomb threat at home, but one might be sent to a major company or building near your home or where you work.

2. Check yes if you feel this type of event could happen. Only complete the remaining fields for those which are checked yes. You can ignore the events checked no.

3. Identify how many times this type of event has happened in the last 5 years.

4. Note the warning signal(s) available for this type of disaster by checking audio (alarm, radio, television, telephone call, reverse 9-1-1 call, pet, broadcast message/community signal), visual (smoke, flames, natural disaster (tornado, blizzard), flashing lights), smell (smoke, gas, chemical), written (in a newspaper, e-mail, television, internet), or none. Any one disaster might have more than one warning signal. And, keep in mind, not all disasters are going to have a warning system (e.g., 9/11, Oklahoma City, or the Minneapolis bridge collapse). And, be aware, warnings can vary from community to community.

5. Select the timeframe you have to get into a safe place. The shorter the time, the more prepared you need to be before confronted with this disaster.

6. If this event were to happen, what is the worst case impact to your family members?

7. If this event were to happen, what is the worst case impact (percentage of loss) to your property?

8. If this event were to happen, what is the worst case impact (percentage of loss) to your financial stability?

Here are the 46 disasters, in alphabetical order:

Possible Disasters

Review each disaster described below. Decide which you need to consider as part of YOUR emergency plan based on your responses.

Disaster	Could happen?	Times happened in last 5 years	Warning Signal(s)	Time to get safe	Human Impact	Property Impact	Financial Impact
Allergic Reaction – Negative reaction to food, insect bite, plants, etc. that results in the need for medical attention	( ) Yes ( ) No	( ) Never ( ) 10+ ( ) 5-9 ( ) 3-4 ( ) 1-2	( ) None ( ) Audio ( ) Visual ( ) Smell ( ) Written	( ) 10 min or less ( ) 3+ days ( ) 24 hr ( ) 1 hr	( ) None ( ) Death ( ) Major Injury ( ) Minor Injury	( ) None ( ) 100% ( ) 75% ( ) 50% ( ) 25%	( ) None ( ) 100% ( ) 75% ( ) 50% ( ) 25%
Avalanche – Can be a natural or man-made rapid flow of snow	( ) Yes ( ) No	( ) Never ( ) 10+ ( ) 5-9 ( ) 3-4 ( ) 1-2	( ) None ( ) Audio ( ) Visual ( ) Smell ( ) Written	( ) 10 min or less ( ) 3+ days ( ) 24 hr ( ) 1 hr	( ) None ( ) Death ( ) Major Injury ( ) Minor Injury	( ) None ( ) 100% ( ) 75% ( ) 50% ( ) 25%	( ) None ( ) 100% ( ) 75% ( ) 50% ( ) 25%
Bomb Threat – Receive a notice that a bomb has been placed in a specific location and may be scheduled to explode	( ) Yes ( ) No	( ) Never ( ) 10+ ( ) 5-9 ( ) 3-4 ( ) 1-2	( ) None ( ) Audio ( ) Visual ( ) Smell ( ) Written	( ) 10 min or less ( ) 3+ days ( ) 24 hr ( ) 1 hr	( ) None ( ) Death ( ) Major Injury ( ) Minor Injury	( ) None ( ) 100% ( ) 75% ( ) 50% ( ) 25%	( ) None ( ) 100% ( ) 75% ( ) 50% ( ) 25%
Coastal Storms – Storms that produce gale-force winds and precipitation (can be rain or snow). Example: Nor'easters	( ) Yes ( ) No	( ) Never ( ) 10+ ( ) 5-9 ( ) 3-4 ( ) 1-2	( ) None ( ) Audio ( ) Visual ( ) Smell ( ) Written	( ) 10 min or less ( ) 3+ days ( ) 24 hr ( ) 1 hr	( ) None ( ) Death ( ) Major Injury ( ) Minor Injury	( ) None ( ) 100% ( ) 75% ( ) 50% ( ) 25%	( ) None ( ) 100% ( ) 75% ( ) 50% ( ) 25%
Computer – Stolen or destruction of data on your home computer	( ) Yes ( ) No	( ) Never ( ) 10+ ( ) 5-9 ( ) 3-4 ( ) 1-2	( ) None ( ) Audio ( ) Visual ( ) Smell ( ) Written	( ) 10 min or less ( ) 3+ days ( ) 24 hr ( ) 1 hr	( ) None ( ) Death ( ) Major Injury ( ) Minor Injury	( ) None ( ) 100% ( ) 75% ( ) 50% ( ) 25%	( ) None ( ) 100% ( ) 75% ( ) 50% ( ) 25%
Contamination – Examples includes drinking water or food borne contamination such as E. coli, salmonella, etc.	( ) Yes ( ) No	( ) Never ( ) 10+ ( ) 5-9 ( ) 3-4 ( ) 1-2	( ) None ( ) Audio ( ) Visual ( ) Smell ( ) Written	( ) 10 min or less ( ) 3+ days ( ) 24 hr ( ) 1 hr	( ) None ( ) Death ( ) Major Injury ( ) Minor Injury	( ) None ( ) 100% ( ) 75% ( ) 50% ( ) 25%	( ) None ( ) 100% ( ) 75% ( ) 50% ( ) 25%
Civil Disobedience – Demonstrations, marches, meetings, picketing, rallies resulting in disorderly conduct with threat of bodily harm and/or interference with normal operations	( ) Yes ( ) No	( ) Never ( ) 10+ ( ) 5-9 ( ) 3-4 ( ) 1-2	( ) None ( ) Audio ( ) Visual ( ) Smell ( ) Written	( ) 10 min or less ( ) 3+ days ( ) 24 hr ( ) 1 hr	( ) None ( ) Death ( ) Major Injury ( ) Minor Injury	( ) None ( ) 100% ( ) 75% ( ) 50% ( ) 25%	( ) None ( ) 100% ( ) 75% ( ) 50% ( ) 25%
Communications Failure – Your normal method of communication is disabled	( ) Yes ( ) No	( ) Never ( ) 10+ ( ) 5-9 ( ) 3-4 ( ) 1-2	( ) None ( ) Audio ( ) Visual ( ) Smell ( ) Written	( ) 10 min or less ( ) 3+ days ( ) 24 hr ( ) 1 hr	( ) None ( ) Death ( ) Major Injury ( ) Minor Injury	( ) None ( ) 100% ( ) 75% ( ) 50% ( ) 25%	( ) None ( ) 100% ( ) 75% ( ) 50% ( ) 25%

Disaster	Could happen?	Times happened in last 5 years	Warning Signal(s)	Time to get safe	Human Impact	Property Impact	Financial Impact
Documents Missing or Incomplete – Critical documents (Will, Living Will, Trusts, Power of Attorney) are not completed or missing when needed	( ) Yes ( ) No	( ) Never ( ) 10+ ( ) 5-9 ( ) 3-4 ( ) 1-2	( ) None ( ) Audio ( ) Visual ( ) Smell ( ) Written	( ) 10 min or less ( ) 3+ days ( ) 24 hr ( ) 1 hr	( ) None ( ) Death ( ) Major Injury ( ) Minor Injury	( ) None ( ) 100% ( ) 75% ( ) 50% ( ) 25%	( ) None ( ) 100% ( ) 75% ( ) 50% ( ) 25%
Earthquakes – Sudden ground motion or trembling possibly resulting in damage or casualties	( ) Yes ( ) No	( ) Never ( ) 10+ ( ) 5-9 ( ) 3-4 ( ) 1-2	( ) None ( ) Audio ( ) Visual ( ) Smell ( ) Written	( ) 10 min or less ( ) 3+ days ( ) 24 hr ( ) 1 hr	( ) None ( ) Death ( ) Major Injury ( ) Minor Injury	( ) None ( ) 100% ( ) 75% ( ) 50% ( ) 25%	( ) None ( ) 100% ( ) 75% ( ) 50% ( ) 25%
Explosion (of any kind) – Consider explosions caused by propane gas, fuels, fireworks, dynamite, chemicals, etc.	( ) Yes ( ) No	( ) Never ( ) 10+ ( ) 5-9 ( ) 3-4 ( ) 1-2	( ) None ( ) Audio ( ) Visual ( ) Smell ( ) Written	( ) 10 min or less ( ) 3+ days ( ) 24 hr ( ) 1 hr	( ) None ( ) Death ( ) Major Injury ( ) Minor Injury	( ) None ( ) 100% ( ) 75% ( ) 50% ( ) 25%	( ) None ( ) 100% ( ) 75% ( ) 50% ( ) 25%
Fire – House (contained or limited) – Fire contained in one house or limited units in a complex	( ) Yes ( ) No	( ) Never ( ) 10+ ( ) 5-9 ( ) 3-4 ( ) 1-2	( ) None ( ) Audio ( ) Visual ( ) Smell ( ) Written	( ) 10 min or less ( ) 3+ days ( ) 24 hr ( ) 1 hr	( ) None ( ) Death ( ) Major Injury ( ) Minor Injury	( ) None ( ) 100% ( ) 75% ( ) 50% ( ) 25%	( ) None ( ) 100% ( ) 75% ( ) 50% ( ) 25%
Fire – Wildfire/Widespread – An uncontrolled fire burning large geographical areas	( ) Yes ( ) No	( ) Never ( ) 10+ ( ) 5-9 ( ) 3-4 ( ) 1-2	( ) None ( ) Audio ( ) Visual ( ) Smell ( ) Written	( ) 10 min or less ( ) 3+ days ( ) 24 hr ( ) 1 hr	( ) None ( ) Death ( ) Major Injury ( ) Minor Injury	( ) None ( ) 100% ( ) 75% ( ) 50% ( ) 25%	( ) None ( ) 100% ( ) 75% ( ) 50% ( ) 25%
Floods – Excessive water (from snowmelt, rainfall or storm surge) overflowing onto the banks and flood plains	( ) Yes ( ) No	( ) Never ( ) 10+ ( ) 5-9 ( ) 3-4 ( ) 1-2	( ) None ( ) Audio ( ) Visual ( ) Smell ( ) Written	( ) 10 min or less ( ) 3+ days ( ) 24 hr ( ) 1 hr	( ) None ( ) Death ( ) Major Injury ( ) Minor Injury	( ) None ( ) 100% ( ) 75% ( ) 50% ( ) 25%	( ) None ( ) 100% ( ) 75% ( ) 50% ( ) 25%
Gas Leak – A disaster where any type of gas is leaking and may create physical harm or death	( ) Yes ( ) No	( ) Never ( ) 10+ ( ) 5-9 ( ) 3-4 ( ) 1-2	( ) None ( ) Audio ( ) Visual ( ) Smell ( ) Written	( ) 10 min or less ( ) 3+ days ( ) 24 hr ( ) 1 hr	( ) None ( ) Death ( ) Major Injury ( ) Minor Injury	( ) None ( ) 100% ( ) 75% ( ) 50% ( ) 25%	( ) None ( ) 100% ( ) 75% ( ) 50% ( ) 25%
Hazardous Materials Spill – Spilling of hazardous materials possibly during transportation or by mistake	( ) Yes ( ) No	( ) Never ( ) 10+ ( ) 5-9 ( ) 3-4 ( ) 1-2	( ) None ( ) Audio ( ) Visual ( ) Smell ( ) Written	( ) 10 min or less ( ) 3+ days ( ) 24 hr ( ) 1 hr	( ) None ( ) Death ( ) Major Injury ( ) Minor Injury	( ) None ( ) 100% ( ) 75% ( ) 50% ( ) 25%	( ) None ( ) 100% ( ) 75% ( ) 50% ( ) 25%
Health Epidemic and/or Infestation – A health scare such as SARs or West Nile Virus	( ) Yes ( ) No	( ) Never ( ) 10+ ( ) 5-9 ( ) 3-4 ( ) 1-2	( ) None ( ) Audio ( ) Visual ( ) Smell ( ) Written	( ) 10 min or less ( ) 3+ days ( ) 24 hr ( ) 1 hr	( ) None ( ) Death ( ) Major Injury ( ) Minor Injury	( ) None ( ) 100% ( ) 75% ( ) 50% ( ) 25%	( ) None ( ) 100% ( ) 75% ( ) 50% ( ) 25%
High Winds – Winds that blow at more than 30 mph and can cause destruction	( ) Yes ( ) No	( ) Never ( ) 10+ ( ) 5-9 ( ) 3-4 ( ) 1-2	( ) None ( ) Audio ( ) Visual ( ) Smell ( ) Written	( ) 10 min or less ( ) 3+ days ( ) 24 hr ( ) 1 hr	( ) None ( ) Death ( ) Major Injury ( ) Minor Injury	( ) None ( ) 100% ( ) 75% ( ) 50% ( ) 25%	( ) None ( ) 100% ( ) 75% ( ) 50% ( ) 25%

Disaster	Could happen?	Times happened in last 5 years	Warning Signal(s)	Time to get safe	Human Impact	Property Impact	Financial Impact
Home Invasion/Robbery – Entry into your home by someone who is not authorized and/or the taking of any asset without permission	( ) Yes ( ) No	( ) Never ( ) 10+ ( ) 5-9 ( ) 3-4 ( ) 1-2	( ) None ( ) Audio ( ) Visual ( ) Smell ( ) Written	( ) 10 min or less ( ) 3+ days ( ) 24 hr ( ) 1 hr	( ) None ( ) Death ( ) Major Injury ( ) Minor Injury	( ) None ( ) 100% ( ) 75% ( ) 50% ( ) 25%	( ) None ( ) 100% ( ) 75% ( ) 50% ( ) 25%
Home System failure – The failure of major home systems such as heating, air conditioning, bursting water pipes, etc.	( ) Yes ( ) No	( ) Never ( ) 10+ ( ) 5-9 ( ) 3-4 ( ) 1-2	( ) None ( ) Audio ( ) Visual ( ) Smell ( ) Written	( ) 10 min or less ( ) 3+ days ( ) 24 hr ( ) 1 hr	( ) None ( ) Death ( ) Major Injury ( ) Minor Injury	( ) None ( ) 100% ( ) 75% ( ) 50% ( ) 25%	( ) None ( ) 100% ( ) 75% ( ) 50% ( ) 25%
Hurricanes – Torrential rains and high winds	( ) Yes ( ) No	( ) Never ( ) 10+ ( ) 5-9 ( ) 3-4 ( ) 1-2	( ) None ( ) Audio ( ) Visual ( ) Smell ( ) Written	( ) 10 min or less ( ) 3+ days ( ) 24 hr ( ) 1 hr	( ) None ( ) Death ( ) Major Injury ( ) Minor Injury	( ) None ( ) 100% ( ) 75% ( ) 50% ( ) 25%	( ) None ( ) 100% ( ) 75% ( ) 50% ( ) 25%
Identity Theft – The unauthorized taking and/or using of your name, personal information, and financial information for purposes of illegal transactions or activities	( ) Yes ( ) No	( ) Never ( ) 10+ ( ) 5-9 ( ) 3-4 ( ) 1-2	( ) None ( ) Audio ( ) Visual ( ) Smell ( ) Written	( ) 10 min or less ( ) 3+ days ( ) 24 hr ( ) 1 hr	( ) None ( ) Death ( ) Major Injury ( ) Minor Injury	( ) None ( ) 100% ( ) 75% ( ) 50% ( ) 25%	( ) None ( ) 100% ( ) 75% ( ) 50% ( ) 25%
Landslides - Can be a natural or man made rapid flow of mud down the side of a hill or mountain	( ) Yes ( ) No	( ) Never ( ) 10+ ( ) 5-9 ( ) 3-4 ( ) 1-2	( ) None ( ) Audio ( ) Visual ( ) Smell ( ) Written	( ) 10 min or less ( ) 3+ days ( ) 24 hr ( ) 1 hr	( ) None ( ) Death ( ) Major Injury ( ) Minor Injury	( ) None ( ) 100% ( ) 75% ( ) 50% ( ) 25%	( ) None ( ) 100% ( ) 75% ( ) 50% ( ) 25%
Lightening - Hits to the earth by lightening (happens at 800 times per minute worldwide)	( ) Yes ( ) No	( ) Never ( ) 10+ ( ) 5-9 ( ) 3-4 ( ) 1-2	( ) None ( ) Audio ( ) Visual ( ) Smell ( ) Written	( ) 10 min or less ( ) 3+ days ( ) 24 hr ( ) 1 hr	( ) None ( ) Death ( ) Major Injury ( ) Minor Injury	( ) None ( ) 100% ( ) 75% ( ) 50% ( ) 25%	( ) None ( ) 100% ( ) 75% ( ) 50% ( ) 25%
Loss of Job – You lose your job, paycheck and benefits due to layoffs, outsourcing, company closing, disaster, etc.	( ) Yes ( ) No	( ) Never ( ) 10+ ( ) 5-9 ( ) 3-4 ( ) 1-2	( ) None ( ) Audio ( ) Visual ( ) Smell ( ) Written	( ) 10 min or less ( ) 3+ days ( ) 24 hr ( ) 1 hr	( ) None ( ) Death ( ) Major Injury ( ) Minor Injury	( ) None ( ) 100% ( ) 75% ( ) 50% ( ) 25%	( ) None ( ) 100% ( ) 75% ( ) 50% ( ) 25%
National Terrorism Alert System – Change in the national terrorism alert system (up or down)	( ) Yes ( ) No	( ) Never ( ) 10+ ( ) 5-9 ( ) 3-4 ( ) 1-2	( ) None ( ) Audio ( ) Visual ( ) Smell ( ) Written	( ) 10 min or less ( ) 3+ days ( ) 24 hr ( ) 1 hr	( ) None ( ) Death ( ) Major Injury ( ) Minor Injury	( ) None ( ) 100% ( ) 75% ( ) 50% ( ) 25%	( ) None ( ) 100% ( ) 75% ( ) 50% ( ) 25%
Nuclear and Radiological Attack/Accident – The discharge of materials or substances that pose a risk to life, health or property if released	( ) Yes ( ) No	( ) Never ( ) 10+ ( ) 5-9 ( ) 3-4 ( ) 1-2	( ) None ( ) Audio ( ) Visual ( ) Smell ( ) Written	( ) 10 min or less ( ) 3+ days ( ) 24 hr ( ) 1 hr	( ) None ( ) Death ( ) Major Injury ( ) Minor Injury	( ) None ( ) 100% ( ) 75% ( ) 50% ( ) 25%	( ) None ( ) 100% ( ) 75% ( ) 50% ( ) 25%

Disaster	Could happen?	Times happened in last 5 years	Warning Signal(s)	Time to get safe	Human Impact	Property Impact	Financial Impact
Safety System Failure – When a disaster occurs, the public or private notification system is rendered inoperable	( ) Yes ( ) No	( ) Never ( ) 10+ ( ) 5-9 ( ) 3-4 ( ) 1-2	( ) None ( ) Audio ( ) Visual ( ) Smell ( ) Written	( ) 10 min or less ( ) 3+ days ( ) 24 hr ( ) 1 hr	( ) None ( ) Death ( ) Major Injury ( ) Minor Injury	( ) None ( ) 100% ( ) 75% ( ) 50% ( ) 25%	( ) None ( ) 100% ( ) 75% ( ) 50% ( ) 25%
Severe Weather – Blizzard or Ice – A storm that creates a hazardous situation with excessive snow and/or ice	( ) Yes ( ) No	( ) Never ( ) 10+ ( ) 5-9 ( ) 3-4 ( ) 1-2	( ) None ( ) Audio ( ) Visual ( ) Smell ( ) Written	( ) 10 min or less ( ) 3+ days ( ) 24 hr ( ) 1 hr	( ) None ( ) Death ( ) Major Injury ( ) Minor Injury	( ) None ( ) 100% ( ) 75% ( ) 50% ( ) 25%	( ) None ( ) 100% ( ) 75% ( ) 50% ( ) 25%
Severe Weather – Extreme Heat or Draught – A period of time in which temperatures rise above the normal levels creating an extreme heat	( ) Yes ( ) No	( ) Never ( ) 10+ ( ) 5-9 ( ) 3-4 ( ) 1-2	( ) None ( ) Audio ( ) Visual ( ) Smell ( ) Written	( ) 10 min or less ( ) 3+ days ( ) 24 hr ( ) 1 hr	( ) None ( ) Death ( ) Major Injury ( ) Minor Injury	( ) None ( ) 100% ( ) 75% ( ) 50% ( ) 25%	( ) None ( ) 100% ( ) 75% ( ) 50% ( ) 25%
Stranded – One or more persons cutoff from others with (or without) life-preserving necessities for the weather or situation	( ) Yes ( ) No	( ) Never ( ) 10+ ( ) 5-9 ( ) 3-4 ( ) 1-2	( ) None ( ) Audio ( ) Visual ( ) Smell ( ) Written	( ) 10 min or less ( ) 3+ days ( ) 24 hr ( ) 1 hr	( ) None ( ) Death ( ) Major Injury ( ) Minor Injury	( ) None ( ) 100% ( ) 75% ( ) 50% ( ) 25%	( ) None ( ) 100% ( ) 75% ( ) 50% ( ) 25%
Terrorist Attack – An attack of any kind by a one or more persons meant to harm assets and/or humans to create fear	( ) Yes ( ) No	( ) Never ( ) 10+ ( ) 5-9 ( ) 3-4 ( ) 1-2	( ) None ( ) Audio ( ) Visual ( ) Smell ( ) Written	( ) 10 min or less ( ) 3+ days ( ) 24 hr ( ) 1 hr	( ) None ( ) Death ( ) Major Injury ( ) Minor Injury	( ) None ( ) 100% ( ) 75% ( ) 50% ( ) 25%	( ) None ( ) 100% ( ) 75% ( ) 50% ( ) 25%
Tornado – A rotating column of air that touches the ground	( ) Yes ( ) No	( ) Never ( ) 10+ ( ) 5-9 ( ) 3-4 ( ) 1-2	( ) None ( ) Audio ( ) Visual ( ) Smell ( ) Written	( ) 10 min or less ( ) 3+ days ( ) 24 hr ( ) 1 hr	( ) None ( ) Death ( ) Major Injury ( ) Minor Injury	( ) None ( ) 100% ( ) 75% ( ) 50% ( ) 25%	( ) None ( ) 100% ( ) 75% ( ) 50% ( ) 25%
Transportation Accident – Air – A disaster involving an airliner, major airport, or any type of flying device	( ) Yes ( ) No	( ) Never ( ) 10+ ( ) 5-9 ( ) 3-4 ( ) 1-2	( ) None ( ) Audio ( ) Visual ( ) Smell ( ) Written	( ) 10 min or less ( ) 3+ days ( ) 24 hr ( ) 1 hr	( ) None ( ) Death ( ) Major Injury ( ) Minor Injury	( ) None ( ) 100% ( ) 75% ( ) 50% ( ) 25%	( ) None ( ) 100% ( ) 75% ( ) 50% ( ) 25%
Transportation Accident – Boat – A disaster involving a cruise ship, personal boat, any water craft, or dock/port	( ) Yes ( ) No	( ) Never ( ) 10+ ( ) 5-9 ( ) 3-4 ( ) 1-2	( ) None ( ) Audio ( ) Visual ( ) Smell ( ) Written	( ) 10 min or less ( ) 3+ days ( ) 24 hr ( ) 1 hr	( ) None ( ) Death ( ) Major Injury ( ) Minor Injury	( ) None ( ) 100% ( ) 75% ( ) 50% ( ) 25%	( ) None ( ) 100% ( ) 75% ( ) 50% ( ) 25%
Transportation Accident – Car/Truck – A disaster involving a car or truck; includes motorcycles, all-terrain vehicles, etc. or major infrastructure	( ) Yes ( ) No	( ) Never ( ) 10+ ( ) 5-9 ( ) 3-4 ( ) 1-2	( ) None ( ) Audio ( ) Visual ( ) Smell ( ) Written	( ) 10 min or less ( ) 3+ days ( ) 24 hr ( ) 1 hr	( ) None ( ) Death ( ) Major Injury ( ) Minor Injury	( ) None ( ) 100% ( ) 75% ( ) 50% ( ) 25%	( ) None ( ) 100% ( ) 75% ( ) 50% ( ) 25%

Disaster	Could happen?	Times happened in last 5 years	Warning Signal(s)	Time to get safe	Human Impact	Property Impact	Financial Impact
Transportation Accident – Rail – A disaster involving a rail system or infrastructure	( ) Yes ( ) No	( ) Never ( ) 10+ ( ) 5-9 ( ) 3-4 ( ) 1-2	( ) None ( ) Audio ( ) Visual ( ) Smell ( ) Written	( ) 10 min or less ( ) 3+ days ( ) 24 hr ( ) 1 hr	( ) None ( ) Death ( ) Major Injury ( ) Minor Injury	( ) None ( ) 100% ( ) 75% ( ) 50% ( ) 25%	( ) None ( ) 100% ( ) 75% ( ) 50% ( ) 25%
Tsunamis – Long, large wave hitting the land	( ) Yes ( ) No	( ) Never ( ) 10+ ( ) 5-9 ( ) 3-4 ( ) 1-2	( ) None ( ) Audio ( ) Visual ( ) Smell ( ) Written	( ) 10 min or less ( ) 3+ days ( ) 24 hr ( ) 1 hr	( ) None ( ) Death ( ) Major Injury ( ) Minor Injury	( ) None ( ) 100% ( ) 75% ( ) 50% ( ) 25%	( ) None ( ) 100% ( ) 75% ( ) 50% ( ) 25%
Unexpected Death – Adult – Death of an adult from an accident or the quick onset of a medical problem leaving little time to prepare	( ) Yes ( ) No	( ) Never ( ) 10+ ( ) 5-9 ( ) 3-4 ( ) 1-2	( ) None ( ) Audio ( ) Visual ( ) Smell ( ) Written	( ) 10 min or less ( ) 3+ days ( ) 24 hr ( ) 1 hr	( ) None ( ) Death ( ) Major Injury ( ) Minor Injury	( ) None ( ) 100% ( ) 75% ( ) 50% ( ) 25%	( ) None ( ) 100% ( ) 75% ( ) 50% ( ) 25%
Unexpected Death – Child – Death of a child from an accident or the quick onset of a medical problem leaving little time to prepare	( ) Yes ( ) No	( ) Never ( ) 10+ ( ) 5-9 ( ) 3-4 ( ) 1-2	( ) None ( ) Audio ( ) Visual ( ) Smell ( ) Written	( ) 10 min or less ( ) 3+ days ( ) 24 hr ( ) 1 hr	( ) None ( ) Death ( ) Major Injury ( ) Minor Injury	( ) None ( ) 100% ( ) 75% ( ) 50% ( ) 25%	( ) None ( ) 100% ( ) 75% ( ) 50% ( ) 25%
Utility Outage –Loss of any utility (electric, gas, water) for more than 4 hours (local or widespread)	( ) Yes ( ) No	( ) Never ( ) 10+ ( ) 5-9 ( ) 3-4 ( ) 1-2	( ) None ( ) Audio ( ) Visual ( ) Smell ( ) Written	( ) 10 min or less ( ) 3+ days ( ) 24 hr ( ) 1 hr	( ) None ( ) Death ( ) Major Injury ( ) Minor Injury	( ) None ( ) 100% ( ) 75% ( ) 50% ( ) 25%	( ) None ( ) 100% ( ) 75% ( ) 50% ( ) 25%
Vicious Animal Attack – Attack on a human by a domesticated or wild animal	( ) Yes ( ) No	( ) Never ( ) 10+ ( ) 5-9 ( ) 3-4 ( ) 1-2	( ) None ( ) Audio ( ) Visual ( ) Smell ( ) Written	( ) 10 min or less ( ) 3+ days ( ) 24 hr ( ) 1 hr	( ) None ( ) Death ( ) Major Injury ( ) Minor Injury	( ) None ( ) 100% ( ) 75% ( ) 50% ( ) 25%	( ) None ( ) 100% ( ) 75% ( ) 50% ( ) 25%
Volcanoes – Magma, gases and ash erupting from a mountain	( ) Yes ( ) No	( ) Never ( ) 10+ ( ) 5-9 ( ) 3-4 ( ) 1-2	( ) None ( ) Audio ( ) Visual ( ) Smell ( ) Written	( ) 10 min or less ( ) 3+ days ( ) 24 hr ( ) 1 hr	( ) None ( ) Death ( ) Major Injury ( ) Minor Injury	( ) None ( ) 100% ( ) 75% ( ) 50% ( ) 25%	( ) None ( ) 100% ( ) 75% ( ) 50% ( ) 25%
Vandalism – An attack on assets such as a home or car	( ) Yes ( ) No	( ) Never ( ) 10+ ( ) 5-9 ( ) 3-4 ( ) 1-2	( ) None ( ) Audio ( ) Visual ( ) Smell ( ) Written	( ) 10 min or less ( ) 3+ days ( ) 24 hr ( ) 1 hr	( ) None ( ) Death ( ) Major Injury ( ) Minor Injury	( ) None ( ) 100% ( ) 75% ( ) 50% ( ) 25%	( ) None ( ) 100% ( ) 75% ( ) 50% ( ) 25%
War – Fighting between more than one country	( ) Yes ( ) No	( ) Never ( ) 10+ ( ) 5-9 ( ) 3-4 ( ) 1-2	( ) None ( ) Audio ( ) Visual ( ) Smell ( ) Written	( ) 10 min or less ( ) 3+ days ( ) 24 hr ( ) 1 hr	( ) None ( ) Death ( ) Major Injury ( ) Minor Injury	( ) None ( ) 100% ( ) 75% ( ) 50% ( ) 25%	( ) None ( ) 100% ( ) 75% ( ) 50% ( ) 25%
Work Stoppage – A group refuses to do their job. Examples: garbage collectors, dock workers, teachers, medical personnel, airline pilots, adult/child day-care, etc.	( ) Yes ( ) No	( ) Never ( ) 10+ ( ) 5-9 ( ) 3-4 ( ) 1-2	( ) None ( ) Audio ( ) Visual ( ) Smell ( ) Written	( ) 10 min or less ( ) 3+ days ( ) 24 hr ( ) 1 hr	( ) None ( ) Death ( ) Major Injury ( ) Minor Injury	( ) None ( ) 100% ( ) 75% ( ) 50% ( ) 25%	( ) None ( ) 100% ( ) 75% ( ) 50% ( ) 25%

Now, it's your turn. Be sure to add any specific disasters that could be faced by your family, based on where you live and your family's configuration, that are not currently on this list. And feel free to email me at my company's e-mail address of <u>info@fundamentalwrites.com</u> so the information can be shared.

Alternate reason

For those of you who may be thinking nothing will ever happen to you, here's an alternate reason for undertaking this exercise.

If you happen to be selling your home, you could use the community information as a marketing tool to illustrate to prospective buyers how much safer and more secure your home is – something to which everyone can relate, and that may just help you with the selling process. Conversely, if you are looking to purchase a new home, you may want to check these issues to be sure the home and community you are considering provide the level of protection you are seeking.

Phase 1 of preparing your customized emergency plan is now complete. At this point, you should have a clear understanding of those disasters which pose a risk to you and your family. You should understand the potential impact these can have on the lives of family members, your property, and your finances. Most importantly, it should be obvious that terrorism and natural disasters are not the only events that you need to address in terms of preparation, survival knowledge, and a recovery plan.

Let's put this list aside for now, and get started on writing *your* emergency plan.

PHASE 2

Writing Your Plan

The writing of your plan starts simply, by defining the scope of your plan. That is, who is covered, and the address of the home you are covering. And it remains simple. In this phase, you will be presented with 14 different loss scenarios called *action plans*. For each one, first determine if it applies to your situation. For example, if you don't have any pets, you can skip the *Loss of a Pet Action Plan* and move to the next plan. Once you have determined that you need a specific action plan, you then write the steps you must do to prepare for, react to, and recover from the loss.

As you add steps to your plan of action, you may realize you need additional information. For example, if you lose your home (no matter the reason), one of your steps you need to take will be to call your insurance agent. To do that, you need their contact details (name, telephone number, etc.) and your policy number. This additional information is what I term a *resource*. For each step you list, determine if there are any resources you need to complete the step. At this point, you have two choices: simply identify these resources and collect this when you get to *Phase 3 – Collecting* or if you have the information readily available, add it immediately to your action plan. In the next section, you will be instructed on how best to obtain and organize all of your resources.

So, in Phase 2, your goal is threefold:

- Set the scope of your plan;
- Determine which loss scenarios fit your family's situation, and write the steps for your action plan;
- Identify the resources you need to complete each step.

You are now ready to begin writing your plan.

3

Setting the Scope

The way to get started is to quit talking and begin doing.
WALT DISNEY

The first step in writing your emergency plan is to define who and what is covered. This is the *scope* of your family plan. Having a well-defined scope helps you stay focused.

Location

Most of us only have one home. This is the place where we live – our primary residence. We can either rent, be purchasing (through a mortgage), or own the home outright.

Others may have multiple homes – a main home and one or more secondary residences, vacation homes, or investment properties used for rental income.

In addition, some people may have family members living next door, upstairs, or nearby in the same community.

For the purposes of writing your plan, you need to select only one location – your primary residence. Why?

Each location is unique, with different combinations of occupants and household contents. There might be different first responders (police, fire, and medical services), and possibly different community warning systems for each area.

Having said that, if you are fortunate enough to have more than one home that is only occupied when you are there, you need a plan for each of your homes.

Once you have selected the location for your plan, take a piece of paper and enter the following information:

- **Family Name** – enter your family's last name. If you have an assortment of last names, enter them as Smith/Jones/Owen, etc.
- **Address** – enter the street address of the location selected. If there is a specific unit number, enter it.
- **City/State/Province/Country** – enter the specifics for the location selected.

Illustration

Here is an example of a layout for this form:

Emergency Plan

Prepared for:

_____

(Family name)

_____

(Address)

_____

(City, state / province, postal code, country)

OK. That wasn't so bad. By completing this page, you have started your emergency plan. Good going!

Who is covered

You now need to define who makes up *your* household. This is rather simple, since it includes all living bodies at the address you just identified. These members can be categorized into one of the following groups:

- **Full-time members** – these are members who live at this address 51% or more of the time. This includes any adult or any child. These members can be assigned tasks to complete when different events occur.

- **Part-time members** – these are members who live at this address 50% or less of the time. These family members should not be assigned specific tasks because they may not be available most of the time. But, part-time members must be knowledgeable about the emergency plan. Examples of part-time members include:
    o College students (home only during vacation periods)
    o A temporary custody situation (whereby a child is at this address for extended periods, but this is not their primary residence)
    o Traveling adults (any adult traveling 51% or more for work and/or fun) e.g., flight attendants, salespersons, technicians, etc.
    o Visiting family members (relatives visiting for extended periods of time). This can include grandchildren or parents who come for extended summer visits.

- **Pets** – all pets that are cared for at the designated location

Illustration

Here is an example of a layout for this form:

Plan Members

Family Coordinator: _____

Backup Coordinator: _____

Family Members Covered*
_____
_____
_____
_____
_____
_____
_____
_____

Part-Time Members
Covered**
_____
_____
_____
_____

Pets
_____
_____
_____
_____

*   List all members who live in the residence 51% or more of their time.

**   List family members who live 50% of less of their time at this residence. This can include family members who are away at school, elderly family members or children who live part time some place else, members who travel for business, etc.

Now it's time to compile your list. Divide your page into full-time, part-time, and pets. Then, write down the names of every family or household member under the relevant category.

Even if you live by yourself, you still need to make a list. Why? As you can see from the example, I have a specific space for a backup person. This can be another family member, or a friend. Your backup should be able to step in to complete your emergency plan should you be unable to do so. If you live a great distance from your family, you may want to select a friend who lives in your area to assist you. The backup person needs to know of the existence of your plan, and will be the main contact for your family. You both might find it beneficial if you were <u>their</u> backup person.

Alternate benefit

By keeping your list up-to-date, you can use it as a check to ensure that your insurance covers everyone who is part of your household. As you add new members (births, adoptions, marriages, etc.), lose other members (divorce, death, marriage/move out, etc.), and still others move from part-time to full-time status (or vice versa), you can check your insurance coverage to be sure it is adequate for your current situation. If you have added a pet, insurance may become a priority for them as well.

The scope of your plan is now set. As you move forward, keep the location and members you identified as your focus. From this point onward, you only need to determine if the location and members identified are impacted. If they are, complete the loss action plan. If they are not, move to the next one. It's that simple!

You are now ready to prepare your action plans, based on losses. Each one of these will be introduced in a separate chapter.

When you have completed your action plans, Phase 2 of writing your emergency plan will be complete.

4

Loss of Communications

The greatest problem in communication is the
illusion that it has been accomplished.
GEORGE BERNARD SHAW

Being able to communicate, both during and after any disaster, can be critical to your physical and mental well-being. Whether it is the sound of a loved one's voice, or being able to call for a first responder, the ability to communicate can literally be a matter of life and death.

That said, communication relies on working equipment, such as telephones, telephone lines, cell phones and cell phone towers. Keep in mind, not all of these may be working when/if you need them. When writing a communications plan, you need to be realistic. It may take several days before equipment is available to allow you to communicate.

Scenarios

Before beginning the design of your family's communication plan, you need to understand the three scenarios in which having a prepared communications plan becomes important:

- You have experienced a disaster that is confined to your family. This can include a family member suffering a heart attack, someone breaking into your home and attacking the adults, a child suffering an allergic reaction to a bee sting, etc. Normally, your initial communication occurs when you request help from a first responder – generally by calling 9-1-1. In any case, a list of telephone numbers for those first calls needs to be prepared and posted in your home. All full-time and part-time members need to know the location of the list, and which number to call for which situation. Additional contacts may be added who are not first responders, but those who may need to be notified, such as employers, schools, churches, close friends, etc.

- You also need a communications plan for instances where you are not at home during a disaster and do not have access to the list. You need to carry a pocket version of your communications plan at all times.

- If you experience a disaster that renders you unable to speak, you need to be able to communicate with first responders. Your communications plan needs to include detailed information about medications and dosages, special medical problems, your physician and other medical contacts, instructions regarding pets, etc.

In two of the three situations outlined above, a written communications plan puts you ahead of the game:

- If you experience a disaster specific to your family, a land-line and/or cell phone should work, so make the list of contact names and numbers. Keep in mind, if a neighbor has called the first responders (9-1-1), you may now need them to make your second level calls – perhaps to your spouse or a parent to let them know what has happened. Having these numbers posted in an easy-to-find location makes it easy for either your neighbor or first responder to make these second level calls.

- If you are rendered speechless, having a pocket version of your communications plan in your wallet provides your first responders with what could possibly be life-saving information. Every family member should carry one.

- A communications plan may not work if you are caught up in a large disaster. If this happens, all family members should call a designated remote contact if possible, however land-lines and cell towers may be damaged. It may be a few days or even weeks before either is operable, so trying to call anyone in the meantime may be impossible. But what if they are working? Wouldn't you at least want to try? Even if it took more than a day to get through, you'd be so glad you did. The contact would bring peace of mind. You should design a plan so everyone knows who to call, and has their number.

Home version

Let's start your communications plan by taking out a piece of paper. The first part is your home list. Once it is done, you should distribute it to those who need a copy.

There are four sections to your home communications. You should include:

- **Your remote contact.** Include his/her name, address, a minimum of two telephone numbers, cell phone, e-mail address (work and home, if applicable), and other pertinent information. One important note – please be sure to check with this person first and make sure they are agreeable to providing this service. You might even offer to be their remote contact in return.

- **First Responder Numbers.** Write down the numbers to call in case of an emergency for police, fire, and medical. In addition, add the police, fire, and medical non-emergency numbers to be used when you need to contact them for a non-emergency event. One example would be the number to contact the police when you need to file an identity theft report or the fire department number in case you smell gas but are not sure of the source.

- **General/Regular Numbers.** List names, telephone numbers, addresses, and e-mails for the people and places your family members visit frequently. Don't forget:
  - o Information on friends of both children and adults
  - o Work, home, cell, and e-mail contact information for your children's friends' parents
  - o Roommates (of family members) work, cell, and e-mail contact information
  - o Work contacts for each family member (boss's name, telephone number, Human Resources number, including e-mail addresses)
  - o Babysitter contact information
  - o Neighbor contact information (who can check on your home in an emergency)
  - o Relative contact information (grandparents, aunts, uncles, etc.)
- **Location to Meet.** Should a disaster occur that blocks you from your neighborhood, you need to have identified another location to meet up with your family members. You can select another family member's home, a school, store, etc. Everyone needs to be aware of this alternate location.

Questions to ask

As you make your list, ask yourself these questions:

- If I had a medical emergency while home alone, what contact information might be needed in case my neighbor or the police needed to contact my family members?
- If I had an accident and could not speak, is there any information the first responders would need to know immediately such as current medication, allergies, etc.?
- Do I want to give a copy of my contacts to others such as my siblings, grandparents, friends, etc.?
- Where should we all meet if we were unable to get to our home?

Illustration

Here is an example of a home version of your communications plan:

Communications Plan - Contact Page

This plan was last updated on: _____/_____/_____

Please complete the following information about your family's out of state contact:

Out of State contact Name:	
Out of State Address:	
Main Telephone Number:	
Secondary Telephone Number:	
E-mail Address:	
Alternate (local) Meeting Location:	

Police Emergency	911	**Police Non-Emergency**	_____
Fire Emergency	911	**Fire Non-Emergency**	_____
Medical Emergency	911	**Medical Non-Emergency**	_____

Please complete the following information about places your family members go to regularly or medical contact numbers (include pets):

Member Name/Location	Contact Information (contact name, address, and telephone)	Where does this site evacuate for emergencies?
Home:		

Once you have made your list, you should post it in a common area in your home, and all family members should be made aware of its location. I recommend you make multiple copies of this list and take a copy to work, give a copy to any of your part-time family members, send copies to other family members (like grandparents, and those living out of state), and give a copy to your backup person.

Pocket version

The following form has been provided for your convenience. A lot of information is included on this form, but most importantly, it is used as a communications tool for your first responders.

If you make one copy of it, simply complete any parts of the form for which the information is identical for all family members, e.g., address, out-of-town contact details, pet details, etc. When this information has been completed, make copies for each member of your family. Now, complete the information specific to each person. Fill in their:

- Name
- Local Contact and telephone numbers (like a parent's number for children, spouse's name and number, friend's name, etc.
- General Information such as birth date, eye and hair color, medical donor status, religion, etc. You can also identify any medical issues or, possibly, recent surgeries. If you need additional space, use the back of the form.
- Physician/Medication Information with details that are critical for medical attention. Again, if you cannot fit all of your medications on one side, use the back of the form.
- Miscellaneous Information with information on any pets, i.e. veteri-

narian contact information and any medical conditions. Add any other information you would like to provide to first responders should this loved one be rushed to the hospital.

When you are done, fold the forms on the dotted lines and give them to each family member to insert in their wallet.

My Communications Plan Updated: ___/___/___

Name: _____

Address: _____

_____

Local Contact: _____

Telephone: _____

_____

Out of Town Contact: _____

Telephone: _____

_____

Alternate Meeting Location: _____

Sex: M F   Date of Birth: _____/_____/_____

Eye Color: _____ Hair Color: _____

Organ Donor: Y N   Contacts: Y N   Med Bracelet: Y N

On file: Healthcare Proxy: Y N   Living Will: Y N

Religion: _____

Health Insurance: _____

Medical Notes (complete on back if needed):

_____

_____

_____

_____

Physician Name: _____

Physician Contact: _____

_____

Blood Type: _____ Allergies: _____

_____

Medication/Dosages: (complete on back if needed)

_____

_____

_____

_____

_____

_____

Pet instructions:_____

_____

_____

_____

Other:

_____

_____

_____

_____

© 2008 YOUR LIFE, Interrupted

I.C.E.

You may have heard a suggestion to store a contact called *I.C.E.* in your cell phone. I.C.E. stands for *In Case of Emergency,* the idea being that responders can easily find your emergency contact information this way.

While this is a good idea, be aware of the limitations that you should keep in mind. First, the responders must have a way of knowing the cell phone belongs to you. If it has been thrown some distance from your body by some impact, there may be no way they can link it back to you. Second, your cell phone may be damaged or destroyed in the disaster, making it impossible for the responder to look up your *I.C.E.* contact. Third, a responder needs to know how to operate your particular type of cell phone. There are so many brands on the market now, and many of them operate differently. Your responders may be unfamiliar with your particular brand.

So, it is a good idea to add *I.C.E.* to your phonebook, but be aware of the limitations.

Budget-wise options

The cheapest way to maintain a communications plan is to write it down. No special tools or equipment are required, making this a cheap and easy option.

Time-wise options

Instead of keeping a paper list, your first Time-wise options option is to create your form on a computer, print out copies for your home and family members' wallets, and e-mail copies to those who need it. As with all information stored on a computer, ensure you have backup routines in place.

You can also create a backup copy by entering all the details for each contact into your cell phone address book. You will then have the contact information at your fingertips if required. Remember to include names, telephone numbers, and policy numbers when appropriate.

A third Time-wise options option is to enter the information into the address book from your internet provider. Enter these names in a special category (you select the title). After entering all the information, print copies and distribute. This method ensures that the contact information is available from any location – so long as you can access the internet.

Alternate benefit

Use the pocket version of your communications plan as a quick reference card for easy access to the information stored on the form. For example, the list of your current medicines helps when visiting your doctor or a specialist, or if you want to pick up some over-the-counter medications, you can easily check them against your list of medications to make sure there are no adverse reactions.

You have just completed a very important step in your emergency plan. At a minimum, you now have a plan to communicate with family members and responders should disaster strike.

Elizabeth M. Owen

5

Home Evacuation I
Action Plan

It takes as much energy to wish as it does to plan.
ELEANOR ROOSEVELT

This chapter focuses on evacuating your home when notified to do so by authorities because of a threatening event. Generally, you will be given a period of time to gather some belongings, pack the car, secure your home, and head towards a safe location. Most often, you leave not knowing when you will be able to return.

Examples

For this action plan, there will usually be a warning of some sort. Authorities sound the warning alarm, and generally set a recommended timeframe in which to complete the evacuation. Beyond the recommended time, your life and/or property may be in danger. These announcements are generally made via television or radio, or by responders going door-to-door. If there is time, you may sometimes see a warning in writing, for example in a newspaper.

Some examples of this type of evacuation scenario include:

- A wildfire is approaching your neighborhood. The fire department uses their reverse 9-1-1 service to notify you about evacuating.

- A hurricane has been tracked for the last seven days. It is a category five (wind speeds at 155 mph+) and is currently on track to hit your neighborhood in two days. Officials are strongly recommending evacuation. They are urging everyone to take shelter in designated locations at least 100 miles from your city. Officials recommend boarding windows and placing sandbags at all doors if homeowners have the necessary resources available, and shutting off all utilities.

- There is a chemical spill at a plant about 25 miles from your home. The cloud generated from the spill is moving towards your neighborhood. It is expected to arrive in about 60 minutes. Authorities have advised everyone to evacuate to the local high school immediately.

- Your area has endured four days of rain, and the river that runs through town is ready to break its banks. Authorities are telling everyone to get out as quickly as possible and move to higher ground.

Although evacuations like these allow you time to collect a few belongings, be aware that the time allowed to prepare to evacuate may be limited, and you will almost certainly not be told when you will be able to return to your home. The *all clear* is generally given by authorities as soon as possible after the event has occurred or the threat has passed.

Questions to ask

As you create your plan to evacuate your home, you need to ask the following questions:

- Are there any (working) warning systems for this type of emergency?
- In a worst-case scenario, how fast do you think you need to be able to

pack the car and get on your way to a safe location? Your answer should be based on the types of events that occur in your area, the likely warning, and how much time you are likely to have to get to safety.

- If you have to evacuate, what are the critical items you need to take for each family member and pet?

- If told to evacuate, how long is it likely to be before you can return?

- If the events in your area are likely to lead to a recommendation to turn off all utilities, do you have the knowledge and tools to do so?

- If you are told to sandbag your house, do you have the materials and tools to do so?

- Would you ever need to board up the windows, and if so, do you have the materials and tools to do so?

- Could your home be damaged by a falling tree, requiring you to improvise a cover for the large hole in the roof that would result?

- Is there a designated evacuation route in your neighborhood, and if so, is it identified somehow?

- Has your community set up an evacuation center, and does everyone in your family know how to get there?

- Does the evacuation center accept pets? If not, what is the plan for your pets? (NOTE: *The Pets Evacuation and Transportation Standards Act* was recently passed by Congress. It says both your state and local authorities must provide alternate locations that accept pets.)

- Is your pet able to be moved in a crate or carrier?

- If your pet has to remain at home, is there a safe room or alternate area where you can leave them loose with a supply of food and water?

Apply it

The most important question in the above list is the first one. Just how fast do you want to be able to pack your car and be on the road towards safety? Whether you said 10 minutes, 30 minutes, or 2 days, you can easily see how much work you have to do before this plan can work.

As an example, I have my own timeframe set at 15 minutes, and I have determined that I might be kept away for up to 5 days. So, I have pre-packed clothes, toiletries, extra glasses, etc. in a suitcase. I'm not packed ready for vacation – this is just some "stuff" to hold me over. I have also packed some water and foodstuffs in a plastic container. From the first warning, I can have the car packed with the suitcase and supplies kit in 5 minutes.

If the evacuation requires me to turn off all utilities before departing, I have 10 minutes in which to do this. Because I have allocated *only* 10 minutes for this, I have typed up instructions for turning off each utility and placed these, along with the necessary tools, next to the utility shut off valve.

I have written my plan as if I am the only one available to perform all the steps. This way, I know it can all be done within the 15 minutes I have set. And, if I am not at home when the disaster strikes, all the steps necessary are written and in place, together with any tools required, so others can do them without me.

I have elected not to use sandbags in the event of rising water, and I have also decided I don't really need to cover my windows with boards, but this is my choice, based on where I happen to live. If I lived in an area where rising water and high winds from hurricanes and other disasters was more likely, I would probably have these things available. I don't have any pets either, so I don't need to make an alternate plan for pets.

Sample

Here is a sample of a completed home evacuation plan. Remember, it is just an example, whereby I want to be in the car and on the road within 15 minutes, and have chosen to be prepared for up to 5 days absence. You need to select a goal and write the steps that are appropriate for your family's evacuation situation.

Evacuation Action Plan I

Goal: Be able to pack the car with necessary goods (to cover 5 days), secure the house, and be headed to the evacuation center within 15 minutes of receiving the warning.

Step	Who	Action	Resources Needed	
1	Anyone	Activate evacuation of home for **non-immediate** emergency.	▪ Knowledge of warning signal(s) and timeframe	
2	Anyone	Shut off utilities if instructed to do so by authorities: ▪ Gas ▪ Electric ▪ Water	▪ Know location of shutoff valve for gas, electric, and water ▪ Tools to shut off valve located next to valve ▪ Written instructions with tools	
3	Anyone	Pack car with pre-packed kits: ▪ Food/Water ▪ Medical Kit ▪ Clothes and Bedding Kit ▪ Tool Kit ▪ Personal Needs Kit	Pre-packed/Stored (identify location): ▪ Food/Water ▪ Medical Kit ▪ Clothes and Bedding Kit ▪ Tool Kit ▪ Personal Needs Kit	
4	Anyone	Secure house by locking doors and windows	▪ Keys (identify location backup copies kept)	
5	Anyone	Load all family members into car	▪ Car with gas	
6	Anyone	Follow evacuation route to approved location	▪ Knowledge of approved evacuation route ▪ Knowledge of destination ▪ Vehicle in working order with gas	
7	Anyone	Activate other checklists, if needed	Communications Plan Loss of Utilities Loss of Child Member Loss of Home Loss of Household Goods Loss of Critical Records	Shelter in Place Loss of Adult Member Loss of Pet Loss of Transportation Identity Theft Loss of Job/Income

Your turn

As you write your evacuation plan, determine how quickly you want to be in the car and ready to move. Simply write the steps in the order they should be completed. Identify any resources – kits, tools, clothes, etc. – you need to make this happen. Enter resource information if you have it. But, if you don't, you need not worry about collecting the resources right now. You will address resources in Phase 3.

As you write your plan, assign different tasks to different members if you want to. Don't forget to include your pets and their needs, and again, list all resources required for them.

Did you get everything?

So, how are you going to know if you have identified each step, and listed each resource required? Well, since this is one of those life and death action plans, you will be practicing this plan to make sure it works. This is done in Phase 4 – Testing and Maintenance. So don't worry whether you have covered everything right now – you'll be testing it out shortly.

Alternate benefit

Preparing this type of plan allows you to identify the location of, and steps needed to turn off, each utility in your home. If you decide to undertake major renovations, this information may be required. Additionally, if you are selling your home, it can be used to hand off your home to the buyer.

Let's move on to the other type of evacuation you need to be prepared to survive – an evacuation where you are given no time to prepare.

6

Home Evacuation Plan II
Action Plan

You may delay, but time will not.
BENJAMIN FRANKLIN

This type of home evacuation is more critical, because when it happens, there is no time to think about, or prepare for, evacuating. You receive little or no warning, and you have to get out immediately. The most common scenario is a house fire. You must evacuate immediately or you risk losing your life.

Examples

The following are examples of situations where a home evacuation is required with no time to prepare:

- A system, like your furnace, explodes.

- A fire in your house sets off the smoke alarm(s).

- An out-of-control vehicle leaves the road and smashes into your home, destroying your kitchen, dining room, and living room.

- After many days of rain, an old tree falls onto your house, tearing away most of your second floor and allowing the rain to enter your first floor.

Questions to ask

When designing your family's plan for a quick escape, think about the following:

- Are there any (working) warning systems for this type of emergency?
- How fast do I want my family to be able to exit the home and arrive at a safe location?
- Do we have a designated meeting place outside of the house where we will all meet?
- Does everyone in the family know at least two exits from every room?
- Are there any impediments in the house that may prevent any family member from using either the first or second exit from any room? Think about barred windows or bolted doors. Don't forget to include basement exits.
- What if someone isn't able to get out of the house? How will they signal responders as to their location?
- Is there any family member or pet needing assistance to exit?
- Should I take anything with me?

Apply it

Because this plan also deals with a life and death situation, the most important question is how fast do you want your family to be able to exit the home and reach a safe location?

I have set my family's timeframe at 3 minutes, from the point at which we first see, hear, or smell the danger. I have designated at least two exits from every room (which was easy, since I live in a ranch house). If we cannot exit through the normal doorways, because of either smoke or fire, we can open any window for a quick exit. The only exception to this is our basement. If the main stairwell coming up into the kitchen was to be blocked, the only other exit is through a bolted, metal double door. This requires unlocking and pushing upwards, which could be a big problem for any children or elderly people who were in my basement at the time.

Our designated safe spot is the mailbox at the end of our (very long) driveway. This will assure we are out of harms' way.

In case we are unable to get out of any room, we have glow sticks in the windowsills of every window. Simply breaking the stick and placing it in the windowsill will easily direct responders to the correct location if someone is trapped.

Since I live in a ranch-style home, I don't have to concern myself with a member exiting from a second floor (or higher for apartments and/or condos). Further, there are only adults in my household (no children or pets), which means I don't have anyone who may need my help exiting the home.

I don't have any protective bars on any windows, so no tools or instructions are needed to enable people to exit. All doors, except the basement exit mentioned above, are easily unlocked and opened from the inside. The basement door requires a bolt to be pushed to unhitch it, and then must be pushed upwards. All the adults in my household are able to maneuver this door. The garage door can be opened manually.

You should assume that, in this type of evacuation, you won't be able to grab a suitcase and other pre-packed items like you did in the previous home evacuation scenario. Because of this, you should make some upfront plans, just in case. Some of the things that can be done include:

- Having a complete set of keys – house, work, and car – duplicated, and kept at a relative's or friend's house for easy retrieval if necessary. Even if your car is fine, if the house burns, all other sets of keys are likely to be destroyed.

- Sending a copy of this plan and all critical documents to an e-mail account. This can be accessed from anywhere, so long as the internet is available (maybe through your local library or workplace). This should include your communications plan, so you have easy access to the numbers you need to call to notify others of the problem.

- If you are unable to return to the home, consider obtaining assistance from the Red Cross.

Sample

Here is an example of a completed immediate evacuation plan. In this example, I have chosen a timeframe of three minutes in which to evacuate everyone and get to the designated safe meeting point. You should add any additional steps that you believe are appropriate for your family's evacuation process, and select an appropriate timeframe for your family.

Evacuation Action Plan II

Goal: Evacuate the home and report to the designated meeting location within 3 minutes of the warning.

Step	Who	Action	Resources Needed
1	Anyone	Activate evacuation of home for **immediate** emergency.	▪ Knowledge of warning signal (s) and timeframe
2	All	Exit from your current location by using either exit option #1 or #2	▪ Knowledge and trained on 2 exits from <u>each</u> room ▪ Assignments to help pets, elderly, or very young
3	All	Go immediately to the designated meeting location outside	▪ Pre-selected meeting location outside of the home ▪ All members must be trained
4	Anyone	Notify responders of the status of each family member (all accounted for or not)	▪ Plan for members to notify responders if they are trapped
5	Anyone	Work with responders to get medical attention for any family member requiring it	▪ Medical history for all family members ▪ List of medications and allergies ▪ Doctor contact information ▪ Medical insurance contact information
6	Anyone	Work with responders and the Red Cross to secure lodging and clothing for the next 24-48 hours.	▪ Keys for car(s) ▪ Driver's License ▪ Credit Cards (for hotel) ▪ Contact List for work, school, family, friends
7	Anyone	Activate other checklists, if needed	Communications Plan Shelter in Place Loss of Utilities Loss of Adult Member Loss of Child Member Loss of Pet Loss of Home Loss of Transportation Loss of Household Goods Identity Theft Loss of Critical Records Loss of Job/Income

Your turn

Before you commence writing your evacuation plan for this type of scenario, determine how fast you want to be able to exit your home and arrive at your designated safe spot.

Now write down the steps you need to take to make this type of evacuation work for you and your family. It may be a very simple plan – if you see, hear or smell smoke or fire, get out immediately and head to the designated meeting point. Don't forget to include pets or other family members who may need your assistance. If you want to do any preparatory tasks, such as giving a spare set of keys to a friend or relative, just list the resources you will require for now. If you have identified resources and you already have the information, simply add it to this action plan now. You will address gathering the other resources in Phase 3.

Alternate benefit

Again, a benefit that is unrelated to emergencies is that when you sell your home, you can make sure all security devices are in working order. Just being aware they exist and making sure they are operable increases the sale value of your home.

Hopefully you will never have to use either of these evacuation plans. But, if you ever do, think how much more of a chance of survival you have given your family members by preparing these plans. You might have just saved one or all of their lives.

7

Shelter-in-Place
Action Plan

A ship in a harbor is safe, but that is
not what ships are built for.
JOHN A. SHEDD

There could be instances when the authorities will instruct you to *shelter-in-place*. You are told to stay in your home because in these circumstances, venturing out would be more dangerous or harmful. A shelter-in-place order may only last for a few hours or it could extend for several days, as in the event of a major blizzard. In any case, you need to be prepared to stay in your home and survive without any assistance from first responders.

Examples

Some examples of when you may be told to shelter-in-place include:

- A chemical explosion at a plant near your home has released deadly toxins into the air that are headed your way. You are going to be safer in your home until the toxic cloud is gone.

- A convict is on the loose in your area, and authorities have directed everyone to shelter-in-place with the doors locked until the convict is captured.

- A snowstorm has dropped 18" of snow in your area overnight, and you can't get out. Authorities have ordered everyone to stay indoors.

- You were told to evacuate due to an approaching Category 5 hurricane, but you either chose to stay, or were unable to leave and go to the local shelter. Now, authorities have ordered you to shelter-in-place until the storm passes.

- A terrorist has detonated a dirty bomb, and the toxic cloud is expected to pass by your home. It is recommended that you turn off your air conditioner, close all windows, move to the highest point in your home and secure your family in your *safe* room (if you have one) with plastic and duct tape (if these are available).

- A tornado has been observed heading towards your area, and you have only minutes to find shelter. You live in a structure without a basement, and need to take refuge in an interior room with the least possible number of windows.

Questions to ask

Questions to consider when completing your plan for sheltering-in-place include:

- Are there any (working) warning systems for this type of emergency?
- Do you understand how authorities warn everyone they need to shelter-in-place?
- How long do you want to be able to survive in your home without any help from your first responders (police, fire, medical)?

- What if a shelter-in-place order is coupled with a loss of utilities (water, electric and/or gas)?

- Do you know how to build a safe room using plastic and duct tape?

- Do you know the correct plastic and duct tape to purchase?

- Do all family members know where the plastic and duct tape is stored (in case you are not home when the event occurs)?

- Will you need to know how to turn off all utilities for this type of emergency?

- Authorities may instruct you to move to the lowest or highest point in your home, depending on the nature of the event. If you only have one floor (you live in a ranch house, apartment, condo, and/or you don't have a basement), what would you do?

- Does your home provide adequate protection from the natural and man-made disasters identified as a risk? If not, is there an alternate plan? For example, would a single-storey home on a cement slab in Tulsa provide you with adequate protection in the case of a tornado? If not, what would your family do?

Apply it

You may think this particular action plan does not apply to you because you do not live in a snowy location, or there are no chemical plants near you. Please think again.

If you live near any major street or railroad track where transportation of dangerous chemicals occurs, this action plan *does* apply to you and your family. If you live in or near a large city, you may be at greater risk of a terrorist attack. And don't forget the warnings of a potential bird flu epidemic. If it reaches your area, you may be forced to work from home as much as possible and avoid any places where people gather. And, if you live in a home that doesn't provide adequate support for you and your family against known disasters such as tornadoes, hurricanes, fires, etc., you need to complete this action plan to understand the extent to which you are protected, and where there is room for improvement.

Sample

Just as you should be prepared to evacuate your home, you also need to be prepared to shelter in your home until danger passes. Here is a sample action plan for just such a situation. Be sure to select an appropriate timeframe for your family.

Shelter-in-Place Action Plan

Goal: Be able to survive for up to 5 days without any support from first responders and to be able to set up a safe-room if instructed within 15 minutes of the notice.

Step	Who	Action	Resources Needed
1	Anyone	Activate the shelter-in-place emergency action plan	▪ Knowledge of warning signal (s) and timeframe
2	Anyone	**If instructed** to move to the highest floor or lowest floor, do so. If you have one floor, select a room in the interior of the home with the least amount of windows and/or vents.	▪ Food and water supplies for up to 5 days ▪ Medicine for up to 5 days ▪ Selected room on each floor
3	Anyone	**If instructed**, set up safe room using plastic and duct tape to cover all openings	▪ Pre-cut plastic to cover windows, doors, vents, and any other openings ▪ Duct Tape ▪ Scissors to cut tape
4	Anyone	**If instructed**, turn off all air conditioning and/or heating units; close all windows	▪ Knowledge of how to shut off a/c or vents ▪ Tools to shut off a/c or vents, if needed ▪ Ability to close all windows
5	Anyone	**If instructed**, turn off electricity, water, and/or gas	▪ Loss of electricity plan ▪ Loss of water plan ▪ Loss of gas plan
6	Anyone	Notify family, friends, and work/school if necessary	▪ Contact lists ▪ Communications Plan
7	Anyone	Activate other checklists, if needed	Communications Plan Loss of Adult Member Loss of Utilities Loss of Pet Loss of Child Member Loss of Transportation Loss of Home Identity Theft Loss of Household Goods Loss of Job/Income Loss of Critical Records

Your turn

Now it's your turn to put together your shelter-in-place plan. Take a piece of paper and write down all the steps you need to take if authorities recommend you stay in your home. Assign names to each step or task if required. Be sure to set a timeframe for how quickly you want to secure your home against chemical or biological releases.

A word about a safe room

When we were warned to purchase plastic and duct tape by Homeland Security in February 2003, my guess is they were trying to avoid problems from a possible chemical or biological release by terrorists. If you did purchase plastic and duct tape then, you should check to make sure it is the most efficient type, and will provide the best level of protection. You should also be clear on what room you plan to use as your *safe room*.

You will use this room to provide protection against the release of any toxic substance. To prepare a safe room, be sure the plastic you use is 2-4 millimeters (about 1/8 inch) thick. The duct tape should be 2" wide. If possible, select a room that contains a hard-wired telephone. Cut the plastic to cover each opening to the outside, including all windows, doors, vents, etc. Make each piece a few inches wider than the opening. To help expedite the process, write the area that each piece of plastic covers right on the plastic (e.g., window nearest door). Keep the duct tape and plastic handy and make sure everyone in the family knows where they are stored. The goal is to ensure there is a barrier between your family and the contaminant.

I would like to offer a brief note on the limitations of plastic and duct tape. First, depending on the chemical or biological substance released and whether it rises or falls, authorities will instruct you to go to the highest floor in your home or the lowest floor in your home. Second, the plastic and duct tape may not be adequate to repel the substance 100% and/or may only provide protection for a limited time.

If you decide you want to construct a room specifically set up as a safe room in your home (like bomb shelters were constructed after World War II), it can be designed to not only protect you against substances in the air, but also protects during a home invasion, tornados, and other major disasters. The amount of protection in a constructed safe room depends on what you decide is affordable and/or appropriate.

Alternate benefit

If you sell your home, these supplies can be left behind for the new homeowners. Again, the safety aspect is a great selling feature. A constructed safe room adds value to your home.

The next action plan addresses the loss of supply from your utilities.

8

Loss of Utilities
Action Plan

It always seems impossible until it's done.
NELSON MANDELA

U tilities, for the purposes of this book, are electricity, water, and gas. Most of the time, we use these resources without even thinking. The hard-wired (land line) telephone in your home, if you have one, is not being considered a utility.

If you had to do without any of these utilities for an hour or so, it might be an irritation, but you and your family would survive. However if you had to do without them for a day, three days, a week, or possibly longer, the impact would be very different. What if you lost all three? Would this place any of your family members in danger?

Think back to August 2003 and the widespread loss of electricity over the northeastern grid of the United States. The entire area was plunged into darkness, and it was three days before all services were restored. Anything that required the use of electricity was not available, for example, use of credit cards, pumping gas, traffic lights, computers, television/radio, elevators, etc. If you experienced that event, writing this plan should be easy for you. Those of you who did not live through it should consider yourselves lucky, and understand that next time, it could be happen where you live.

Examples

Here are a few examples of the loss of one or more utilities, and the effects this can have:

- Major construction is going on in or near your neighborhood. The water company has notified all residents that the water will be shut off from 9 am to 3 pm while they install sewer lines.

- On the hottest day of the summer, you suddenly lose power. You are keeping life-saving medicine for a family member in the refrigerator. The maximum time you can do without electricity before this medicine is ruined is 4 hours.

- Your 85-year-old mother lives with you, and it is critical she has air conditioning in the summer and heat in the winter. One winter's night a storm sweeps through your area and knocks out the power. The maximum time you can do without electricity before she is impacted is 2 hours.

- After a massive snowstorm, you are asked to shelter-in-place by authorities. You have no running water, no gas (for heat), and no electricity. You are able to cook on the gas grill outside, using bottled gas, you have water stored in your emergency supply kit, and you use your fireplace, layers of clothes, and blankets to keep warm. You figure you can last for 24 hours at most before this becomes an intolerable situation.

- You return to your home after a level 5 hurricane to begin rebuilding. You have no running water and no electricity. None of your family members (humans or pets) have any pressing medical needs, and you have enough provisions to survive for at least 72 hours. You have water, food, bedding, clothes, and candles in your kit. It's tough without air conditioning, but otherwise you can survive.

- The sewer pipe from the city line into your home has burst, and it is your responsibility to arrange for repairs. You're advised that it will take at least 24 hours before anyone can help.

Questions to ask

The responses to some of these questions will largely depend on the makeup of your family, and on their capacity to withstand heat and/or cold:

- Are there any (working) warning systems for this type of emergency?
- How can you determine if the loss of the utility is widespread, or specific to just your house?
- For each utility, what number do you call to report the problem?
- How long can the entire family (humans and pets) withstand the loss of electricity?
- How long can the entire family (humans and pets) withstand the loss of gas?
- How long can the entire family (humans and pets) withstand the loss of running water?
- Are there any medical issues that will be complicated by the loss of any utilities?
- What if the loss of any or all utilities is combined with a shelter-in-place order from authorities?
- Do you know how to turn off all of these utilities if instructed to do so by authorities?
- Would the impact be different if the loss occurred in the summer months versus the winter months?

Apply it

You can use either the blackout of 2003 or Hurricane Katrina as a basis for determining what you would need to do if either of these events were to happen again. Think of any life-impacting systems or resources requiring electricity, as well as the need to obtain water for survival. Consider everything you do today that makes use of any one of your utilities, and then figure out what you would need to do if that utility was unavailable for a day or more.

Sample

Feel free to use the following example to help you come up with your own steps for a situation when one or more utilities are lost for an extended period of time.

Loss of Utility Action Plan

Goal: Be able to survive for up to 8 hours without electricity, water, or gas during any season.

Step	Who	Action	Resources Needed
1	Anyone	Activate the loss of utilities checklist	▪ Knowledge of warning signal (s) and timeframe
2	Anyone	Determine if you are the only home affected or if this is widespread by talking with neighbors and/or calling the utility	▪ Contact information for water, gas, and electric companies ▪ Knowledge of location of shutoff valve for each utility ▪ Tools for shutting off utility if instructed to do so
3	Anyone	Loss of electricity ▪ Check Fuse Box ▪ Turn off all major appliances (or unplug) ▪ Open/close doors and windows to control temperature in home ▪ Secure perimeter ▪ Limit opening of refrigerator/freezer ▪ Limit toilet flushing	▪ Location of fuse box ▪ Extra fuses ▪ Generator (if critical need) ▪ Flashlights/candles ▪ Frozen ice bags to chill items ▪ Sanitary/Toilet Kit ▪ Battery operated radio
4	Anyone	Loss of water ▪ Limit toilet flushing ▪ Ration water for drinking ▪ Utilize low salt foods (to reduce thirst)	▪ Water Kit ▪ Bleach to purify contaminated water before using ▪ Emergency water supply: ice cubes, water in hot water heater, rainwater, ponds, lakes, rivers, and natural springs
5	Anyone	Loss of gas ▪ Turn off appliance ▪ Evacuate if you smell gas	▪ Know the location of appliance gas shut off valves (versus main valve for your home) ▪ Do NOT shut off main valve unless critical (you should NOT turn main gas valve back on — get a professional)
6	Anyone	Notify family and friends if necessary	▪ Communications Plan
7	Anyone	Activate other checklists, if needed	Communications Plan Evacuation Plan I Loss of Child Member Shelter in Place Loss of Home Loss of Adult Member Loss of Household Goods Loss of Pet Loss of Critical Records Loss of Transportation Loss of Job/Income Identity Theft

Your turn

People without elderly or extremely young family members, or those who have medical issues, may not see this type of loss as severe. They feel that they could easily survive for a few days – maybe a little uncomfortably – depending on the weather. Keep in mind however that widespread loss of electricity means no ATMs or credit card usage, no gas pumps, no electronic entertainment (television, movies or games), no recharging of cell phones, no computers, etc. Loss of gas may mean no hot water or cooking. And lack of water can quickly become a major survival issue. Be sure to enter any resource information you have readily available. Note any other resources for collection during Phase 3.

Alternate benefit

If, at any point in time, you decide to begin a conservation program for any or all of your utilities, you can start with this action plan. You should have identified how to get by without each utility, so there's no reason why you can't start putting these alternate steps into practice. They will save you money, and help conserve precious resources.

In working through this action plan, you may have decided that there would be absolutely no negative impact on family members if you lost these utilities, other than the temporary loss of your favorite entertainment devices.

On the other hand, you may have uncovered a serious risk requiring a solid backup plan should any or all of the utilities be rendered unavailable for an extended period of time. Just think how much better positioned your family will be simply because you prepared this action plan. My hope is that you never need to use it, but if you do, your ability to cope with a few days without utilities will be so much greater – possibly even life-saving – due to this pre-planning.

9

Loss of Adult Family Member Action Plan

No one can confidently say that he
will still be living tomorrow.
EURIPIDES

This part of your plan centers on the family's response to the loss of one or more of the adult members of the family. When thinking about this type of loss, you should consider anything from severe injuries that prevent the family member from performing their normal daily routine, to a situation where someone goes missing or is kidnapped, right up to the death of a family member. In other words, the adult is no longer available to function as they normally would within the family. In all these cases, the family must make a transition to a life, either temporarily or permanently, without this person being able to contribute.

Be sure to complete a separate action plan for each full- and part-time adult member, identifying the steps to be taken should this happen to any one of them.

This chapter may make people squeamish, but let me assure you, it is not just about your death. It's about what happens if you become incapacitated – temporarily or permanently – and are not there for your family on a daily basis. If something happens such that you are unable to function as you normally would, this action plan provides them with written instructions guiding them through the steps they will need to take. They need specific names and numbers of people they need to call at work and/or at school. Which friends and family members would need to be notified? It helps if they are able to call those people quickly, without having to waste time finding the necessary contact details. Further, being able to cancel any scheduled appointments and deliveries that are no longer necessary can be a money-saver. Yes, the worst-case scenario for this action plan is your death, but it also addresses much less serious situations that will also require many of the same steps to be completed. It is likely to be a difficult time for your family should they find themselves needing to use this action plan for any reason. Why not give them a roadmap to help get them through their ordeal?

Examples

The loss of an adult can be either expected or unexpected, and it can be either permanent or only temporary. Examples can include:

- Heart attack or other medical emergency
- Car crash
- Terrorist attack
- Missing person
- A hazing incident on campus
- Injury during a home invasion
- Illness
- Animal attack
- Suicide
- Any kind of accident

Questions to ask

Each adult needs to write a plan for themselves, outlining all the steps the surviving members need to take in this situation. Some questions to ask include:

- Are there any (working) warning systems for this type of emergency?
- Is there *anything* you would need to have done immediately, were you to die unexpectedly or if you were unable to, or unavailable to, act on your own behalf?
- Are you a donor and if so, does your family know?
- If needed, are your funeral wishes clearly spelled out?
- Is money available to pay for a funeral if required (the average funeral runs around $8,000 - $10,000)? If so, where can they find it?
- Do you have a current photo (for a missing person scenario)?
- Does the family know who to call at your place of work to notify them of your situation?
- What financial arrangements does your work provide in the event of death or incapacitation? This includes your paycheck, vacation payout, short-term and long-term disability, and any other benefits due to you and your family.
- Who, among friends and family, needs to be notified in the event of death or serious illness?
- Where are all the critical documents stored, and who can access them?
- Is there any special care needed for pets? This is especially important if you live away from your family.
- What bills need to be paid?
- Are there any *secret* investments, deposits or purchases you need to identify?

- Is there a list of financial vendors who need to be notified? Examples to consider are your mortgage company, car note, bank or credit union, credit card companies, anyone you owe money to (personally), anyone who owes you money (personally), etc.

- Are there any regularly-scheduled appointments that need to be cancelled? If so, where are they recorded? Examples include any type of medical services, massages, therapy of any kind, classes, volunteer visits, pet appointments, etc.

- Which vendors need to be notified to discontinue services and/or automatic delivery of purchases? Examples to consider include cell phone, newspapers, magazines, internet connection, mail, automatic shipments of supplies of any kind (medicine, coffee, contact lenses, pet food, etc.), lawn services, internet services, pool services, electric, gas, water, gutter cleaning services, home heating oil, doctors (for humans or pets), etc.

- Is there any message that needs to be left for family members? This allows you time to prepare a farewell message for family members before anything happens to you.

- What would happen if more than one adult member of the family was lost at the same time? For example, what would happen if both parents were killed in a car crash?

Apply it

When dealing with the loss of an adult member, there are three phases. Initially, there is the notification and realization something has happened. Next, if death is the outcome, the preparation for the farewell ceremony needs to be handled. In the third phase, the surviving members take their first steps towards a life without the departed or incapacitated member.

Notification is generally received from a first responder (fire, police, or medical). Think about what you would want your family to do within the first four hours of being notified. Is there anything they *must* do first? Who needs to be contacted? Write these steps down. Whether or not death is the result, these initial steps are going to be the same.

The next phase, should death occur, is a focus on a farewell ceremony. It may or may not be religious, and it may take place anywhere from within a day of the death to sometimes weeks later. Some people, because of their profile or status, actually have more than one farewell ceremony. Write out what your family needs to do, and who they need to contact, to make the farewell ceremony happen in accordance with your wishes. Again, think about the positive impact this step will have on your family should this be needed.

The transition phase will be associated with financial, legal and property issues. Surviving family members might also be dealing with anxiety or depression, and possibly even varying degrees of incapacity of their own. How does the family move forward without your daily input and contributions?

Finally, you need to think about what you have – and, most importantly, have not – said to family members. Once you are gone, it is too late. So, if you cannot verbalize your feelings, think about writing them down or videotaping a message, so they are left knowing how you felt.

Sample

The action plan for each adult member will be different, but here is an example you can use to get your plan started:

Loss of Adult Member Action Plan

Goal: Be able to follow the steps required should this adult become temporarily or permanently incapacitated.

Step	Who	Action	Resources Needed
1	Anyone	Activate loss of adult action plan	
2	Anyone	Assess the situation • Permanent loss • Temporary loss	• Notification from first responders • Current photo • Insurance coverage (for treatment and hospital fees) • Farewell plans, if appropriate • Access to legal documents (Medical Power of Attorney)
3	Anyone	Notifications	• Contact list for possible adjustments needed: ○ Family members ○ Member's work (boss or Personnel)/School (Principal) ○ Your work (boss or Personnel)/School (your Principal) ○ Member's daily activities (friends, co-workers, others) ○ Your daily activities (friends, co-workers, others)
4	Anyone	Adjusting to temporary loss • Additional notifications • Adjusting daily routines • Adjusting financially • Adjusting living arrangements • Pet care • Anything else to address	• Contact list for possible adjustments needed: ○ Member's regular deliveries (paper, mail, e-mail, etc.) ○ Member's creditors/bill paying (example: auto-bill pay) ○ Any family member's regular activities impacted (piano, soccer, exercise class, Bible class, etc.) ○ Long-term care insurance, if applicable ○ Pet care information • Daily routines outlined (in case all adults are incapacitated)
5	Anyone	Farewell Ceremony • Public Announcement • Body handling arrangements • Burial arrangements	• Member's background for public announcement • Pre-paid arrangements, if any • Ceremony details (music, readings, locations, etc.) • Organ donor card • Death Certificate • After death wishes (must be written)
6	Anyone	After the Farewell Ceremony adjustment • Financial • Daily routine • Living arrangements • Notifications of death • Write Thank You notes • Close out accounts	• Copies of death certificate • Amounts due to whom • Income streams • Appointments to be cancelled • Will • Insurance payouts • Addresses and Thank You cards • List of accounts to close (credit cards, gym, cell, internet, etc.)
7	Anyone	Activate other checklists, if needed	Communications Plan Evacuation Plan I Evacuation Plan II Shelter in Place Loss of Utilities Loss of Pet Loss of Child Member Loss of Transportation Loss of Home Identity Theft Loss of Household Goods Loss of Job/Income Loss of Critical Records

Your turn

Each adult should write their own plan, since they are best placed to know what the family needs to do, and who needs to be contacted, if they are suddenly unable to participate on a daily basis. If you have not yet decided on your funeral arrangements, this may be a good time to consider doing so. Remember, this is done for the benefit of your _surviving_ family members. And if you think your spouse will be able to do it when you are gone, what would the rest of the family do if _both_ you and your spouse were gone?

Consider this your last act of kindness towards your family. When you are gone, the transition is going to be tough enough, so why not make it just a little bit easier on them by outlining the steps they will need to take?

I have a Will and some life insurance so I guess I don't need this type of plan?

I would argue you still need this type of action plan. A Will lays out how your estate is to be distributed, and is often not read until weeks or even months after death occurs. Therefore if an emergency plan has not been completed, your family will be left in the dark and forced to fend for itself during its time of grief. Sure, life insurance will be helpful for the financial transition, but does your family even know the policy exists, and who to contact? In any event, the payout may not be made immediately, so what will they do in the interim period? Having a Will and insurance is a good start but is woefully inadequate for your family's response and recovery.

Alternate benefit

Having a current list of contacts ensures that these critical details are documented and up-to-date in the event you or any other family member needs to contact them for any reason. This includes people like your current boss, your personnel department, your financial information (credit cards, bank notes, etc.) and regularly-scheduled activities (doctors, house maintenance, internet accounts, etc.).

Most of us don't like to even think about our own passing, but this action plan has a dual benefit. First, it is for you, because it makes sure everything you have worked hard to accomplish is handled according to your wishes in the event of your death – whether expected or not. But it is also for your family, because it walks them through what they will need to do when you die. It's a win-win situation.

If you have children for whom you are responsible, the next section of the emergency plan addresses the steps you need to follow should you lose one or more of them. If you don't have any children, you can skip to Chapter 11.

10

Loss of Child Family Member Action Plan

Death is the cure of all diseases.
SIR THOMAS BROWN

It's sad to think about harm being done to any child, let alone the death of a child, yet as you have seen, there are daily forces that place everyone at risk. Although you try your best to protect your children, sometimes things are out of your hands. This plan is about being prepared, just in case. You lay out the steps you need to take if you are confronted with an event including major harm to, or loss of, one or more of your children. Like the plan for any adult, you need to consider anything from illness or injury, through a missing child, right up to and including death when writing this plan for each child.

Examples

If you have children in your household, review the list of possible situations in which a child may be severely harmed or could even die. These include:

- Medical emergency

- Car crash
- Terrorist attack
- Walking away from a family outing and becoming lost
- Drowning in a neighborhood pool
- Separated from family in a natural disaster
- Violence at school
- Gun accident
- Kidnapping

Questions to ask

Again, you need to write a plan for each child, since they each have different friends, may go to different schools, have different after-school activities, etc. Also write a plan for all *part-time* children who are away at school (at any level) or who are cared for under shared arrangements. When writing each child's plan, use the following questions to help make sure all necessary steps are included:

- Are there any (working) warning systems for this type of emergency?
- Is there *anything* that needs to be done immediately if this child dies or is severely impacted?
- Do you want your child to be a donor?
- Is there money available to pay for a funeral (remember, the average funeral runs around $8,000 - $10,000)?
- Who needs to be called at school to notify them of this child's death or severe illness?
- Do you have a current photo of the child (for a missing person scenario)?
- Who should be called if the child has a job? Are there any final pay-

ments, vacation payout, short-term or long-term disability, or any other benefits due?

- Which specific friends and family need to be notified upon the child's death or severe illness?

- Where are the critical documents for this child? Examples may include birth certificate, vaccination record, social security card, license, life insurance, etc.

- Is the care of any pets affected because of the death of, or harm to, this child?

- Are there any secrets which need to be shared if this child should die?

- Are there any financial vendors who need to be notified? Examples to consider are car note, bank or credit union, credit card companies, anyone the child owes money to (personally), anyone who owes the child money (personally), etc.

- Are there any regularly-scheduled appointments which need to be cancelled for this child? If so, where are these recorded? Examples may include any type of medical services, therapy of any kind, classes, volunteer visits, pet appointments, etc.

- Which vendors need to be notified to discontinue services and/or automatic delivery of purchases? Examples to consider include cell phone, newspapers, magazines, internet connectivity, mail, automatic shipment to replenish supplies of any kind (medicine, coffee, contact lenses, pet food, etc.), internet providers, doctors (of any kind), etc.

- Has this child been able to say any final words to each family member?

- What happens if more than one member of the family dies or becomes incapacitated at the same time?

Apply it

As with the loss of an adult, there are three phases when a child dies. First, you are notified of the event, and required to assess the situation. Then there are the tasks needed to say your final goodbye to the child, should death have occurred. Third, you need to begin the transition to life without this child.

Depending on the age of your child, there may be little or no financial, work, school, or other contact required outside your family and friends, but you should think about the steps you would need to complete should they become incapacitated or, worst case, die.

Sample

Should you be confronted with this type of loss, having this type of action plan prepared will make the process a little easier. How? If you were to be confronted with this type of tragedy, you would be required to come up with a plan. So, you can do it while you are in the middle of the catastrophe and the grieving, or you can do it *before* something happens, when you are calm, and able to think rationally. Then, should something happen, you can hand off the action plan to a close friend or other family member to complete while you take care of dealing with what has hit you. Remember, you may be the one responsible for comforting other family members.

It's your choice, but I strongly suggest you prepare a plan.

Loss of Child Member Action Plan

Goal: Be able to follow the steps required should this child become temporarily or permanently incapacitated.

Step	Who	Action	Resources Needed
1	Anyone	Activate loss of a child action plan.	
2	Anyone	Assess the situation • Permanent loss • Temporary loss	• Notification from first responders • Current photo • Insurance coverage (for treatment and hospital fees) • Farewell plans, if appropriate • Legal documents as appropriate

3	Anyone	Notifications	• Contact list for possible adjustments needed:
			  o Family members
			  o Child's work (boss or Personnel)/School (Principal)
			  o Your work (boss or Personnel)/School (your Principal)
			  o Child's daily activities (friends, school/work mates, others)
			  o Your daily activities (friends, co-workers, others)

4	Anyone	Adjusting to temporary loss
		• Additional notifications
		• Adjusting daily routines
		• Adjusting financially
		• Adjusting living arrangements
		• Pet care
		• Anything else
			• Contact list for:
			  o Child's regular deliveries (e-mail, mail, etc.)
			  o Child's creditors/bill paying (example: car note)
			  o Any family member's regular activities impacted (piano, soccer, exercise class, Bible class, etc.)
			  o Long-term insurance coverage, if applicable
			  o Pet care information
			• Daily routines outlined (in case one or more adults are involved)

5	Anyone	Farewell Ceremony • Public announcement • Body handling arrangements • Burial arrangements	• Child's background for public announcement • Pre-paid arrangements, if any • Ceremony details (music, readings, locations, etc.) • Organ donor card • After death wishes (must be written)
6	Anyone	After the Farewell Ceremony adjustment • Financial • Daily routine • Living arrangements • Notifications of death • Write Thank You notes • Close out accounts	• Copies of death certificate • Amounts due to whom • Insurance and income • Appointments to be cancelled • Legal documents • Addresses and Thank You cards • List of accounts to close (gym, internet, cell, etc.)
7	Anyone	Activate other checklists, if needed	Communications Plan Evacuation Plan I Evacuation Plan II Shelter in Place Loss of Utilities Loss of Adult Member Loss of Home Loss of Pet Loss of Household Goods Loss of Transportation Loss of Critical Records Identity Theft Loss of Job/Income

Your turn

You should write a plan for each child in your family. Identify the location of critical papers, and who needs to be contacted. Gather as much information as possible. Remember, if you are too distraught to complete any of these steps should an event occur, a relative or close family friend can take over for you if you have the steps written down.

One note about making your child a medical donor: it is important that you document whether or not this is what you desire. A situation may conceivably arise whereby both parents, along with one or more children, perish. In this case, it is important that whoever is left to take care of things, whether it is family or friends, is aware of your wishes. Don't make this any harder for them than it already is.

Alternate benefit

As part of this plan, you need to collect contact details for your child's current circle of friends, bosses (if they work or baby sit), doctors, and teachers. Having a current contact list for each of your children – and updating it regularly – ensures that you are able to *find* your children quickly should the need arise.

This is a very sad chapter, and I hope you never need to use it. That said, if you ever do, you are now much better prepared to handle the situation and make as smooth a transition as possible. And if the need arises to have someone else complete these tasks because you have also been taken, think how much easier you will be making it for them.

11

Loss of Pet Action Plan

Animals are such agreeable friends – they ask no questions, they pass no criticisms.
GEORGE ELLIOT

So many people have pets living in their homes as valued members of the family. That's why, if you have a pet (or pets), you need to have a plan in the event you lose them, or they fall ill or are injured. Losing a pet can be as disruptive to family life as losing any other family member, so you need to have a plan in place to determine what needs to be done first. Then, you may need a transition plan.

Just as with humans, if you have more than one pet, you need to prepare a plan for each of them.

Examples

The loss of a pet can occur when:

- A medical condition ends the pet's life

- A pet is stolen

- A pet dies as the result of a disaster such as a house fire

- A pet gets hit by a vehicle and is injured or killed
- A pet gets out and is lost

Questions to ask

Use the following questions to help you complete a Loss of Pet plan:

- Are there any (working) warning systems for this type of emergency?
- Does your pet wear an ID tag? If so, does the tag include contact information?
- Have you had a microchip implanted?
- Do you have any current pictures of your pet?
- If a pet was lost, how long would you wait before notifying authorities?
- Do you want to have a farewell ceremony for your pet when they die?
- What would you like to do with your pet's remains?
- If your pet cannot come with you in the event of an evacuation, what is your plan for leaving them in the home?
- Is there anyone who needs to be notified in the event of the pet's death? Examples include any people who provide regular services to your pet, such as their veterinarian, groomer and walker, as well as family members, friends, etc.

Apply it

You need to list the steps required to address the loss of a pet, and as with the loss of an adult or child, the plan is important in the event that all members of your immediate family are gone, and a relative or someone else is left to figure out what needs to be done. It is also important to write a plan for each pet.

Sample

As with any family member, losing a pet can be devastating. Here is an example of a plan of action to use in the event of the loss of a pet.

Loss of Pet Action Plan

Goal: Be able to follow the steps required should this pet become temporarily or permanently incapacitated.

Step	Who	Action	Resources Needed
1	Anyone	Activate loss of pet action plan	
2	Anyone	Assess the situation • Permanent loss (follow farewell planning) • Temporary loss (determine next steps for treatment and recovery)	• Notification from first responders • Current photo • Insurance coverage (for treatment and hospital fees), if appropriate • Farewell plans, if appropriate
3	Anyone	Notifications	• Contact list for: o Family members o Pet's contacts for activity (vet, groomer, walker, etc.) o Your work (boss or Personnel)/School (your Principal) if impacted
4	Anyone	Farewell Ceremony • Body handling arrangements • Burial arrangements	• Pre-paid arrangements, if any • Ceremony details (music, readings, locations, etc.)
6	Anyone	After the Farewell Ceremony adjustment • Notifications of death • Write Thank You notes • Close out accounts	• Appointments to be cancelled • Insurance payouts • Addresses and Thank You cards • List of accounts to close (vet, groomer, caretaker, etc.)
7	Anyone	Activate other checklists, if needed	Communications Plan Evacuation Plan I Evacuation Plan II Shelter in Place Loss of Utilities Loss of Adult Member Loss of Child Member Loss of Transportation Loss of Home Identity Theft Loss of Household Goods Loss of Job/Income Loss of Critical Records

Your turn

List the steps to be taken if your pet becomes incapacitated or dies. Be as detailed as possible. This will enable your family or friends to take proper care of your pet should something happen to you at the same time.

Alternate benefit

Like the loss of an adult or child member, the action plan makes sure contact information is up to date for your pet(s). You never know when another member of the family may need to make contact for whatever reason.

With this chapter, you have now completed a plan to adjust to the loss (or incapacitation) of any family member. In the next few chapters, you address the loss of things such as your home, your household goods, transportation, etc. While the chapters relating to the possible loss of life may have been difficult, the following chapters should be a little less stressful.

12

Loss of Home Action Plan

Not going home is already like death.
E. CATHERINE TOBLER

What would you do if your home was completely destroyed? How would you pick up your life, and go on? The loss of your home, either temporarily or permanently, generally follows on the heels of one of your home evacuation plans. Once everyone is out of the house and safely relocated, and anyone who requires medical attention has received it, you need to turn your attention to where you are going to live.

This plan could be written to address anything from partial loss up to total home loss. I suggest you design the plan for the *worst-case scenario*. That way, anything less will be automatically covered.

The plan is focused on those people who own, or are buying, their own home. If you are renting, the responsibility of cleaning up and repairing, or rebuilding if required, rests with the owner of the property.

Examples

Scenarios where you may lose part or your entire home include:

- Your kitchen catches on fire while you're preparing dinner.

- The furnace explodes while you're out, totally destroying the house.
- In an apartment or condo situation, your neighbor's hot water heater bursts and floods your unit.
- A tree falls on the house during a storm, damaging your second floor and leaving a huge hole in the roof which must be fixed before you can move back in.
- A flood inundates your first floor with mud.
- A tornado blows through town, completely destroying your home.
- While you're on vacation, there is an electrical malfunction and your home burns to the ground.

Questions to ask

As you design a plan for what you will do if your home is damaged or destroyed, you need to ask yourself the following questions:

- Are there any (working) warning systems for this type of emergency?
- Do you have any options for free temporary housing?
- Do your options for free temporary housing change for a 14-day timeframe versus a 30-day timeframe versus a 90-day timeframe?
- How does your plan differ if you suffer a partial loss of your home versus a total loss?
- What are the critical records and information about your home you would need to access soon after the event and where are these kept?
- Do you have tools and materials to temporarily secure your house (e.g., tarps, plastic sheeting, plywood, etc.) in an accessible location?
- What exactly is covered by your homeowner's insurance policy?
- Do you know how to submit a claim with your insurance carrier? What specific information will they require?

- Do you know how to turn off the water, gas, and electricity in your unit or home?

- Do you know how long it would take from submitting a claim until you received a reimbursement check? Would you get more than one check? What would you do until the first check arrived?

- Who are the vendors who bring goods or services to your home on a daily, weekly or monthly basis? Which ones would you continue to use, and which ones would you cancel until you were able to return? Examples include yard services, US mail, overnight delivery services, pool services, utilities and system maintenance (air conditioner, heater, etc.).

- How would *not* living in your home impact your normal daily routines?

- What would happen if the event was widespread, and all of your relatives and friends were faced with the same issues? Would that change this plan?

Apply it

Whatever happens, anything that causes you to be out of your home for a period of time, or even permanently, is going to have some financial impact. You may decide to write a plan whereby you stay in a hotel if something happens, but you need the financial capacity to be able to do this for it to be realistic. In some instances, your temporary accommodation may be covered by insurance – either yours, or that of whoever was responsible for the damage – but the decision and consequent payment of expenses may take a while.

Some people have insurance coverage designed to handle these intermediate costs, while others may have the luxury of using a spare room at the home of a relative or friend. If you don't have the capacity to pay for someplace to stay, and none of these alternatives are available, you may need to think about contacting an organization like the Red Cross for assistance, in which case you should include this step in your plan.

Although the Red Cross can provide assistance for the first few days following an event of this type, you need to have a plan to cover your housing needs beyond that period. Depending on the scope of the event, FEMA (US Federal Emergency Management Agency) may provide assistance in the form of low-interest loans.

Some of your choices may depend on your daily routine and habits, which may prevent you from moving too far from your current home, assuming it is not a widespread disaster.

Sample

We have all seen this situation played out on our televisions, when we witnessed the effects of Hurricanes Katrina and Rita. Use the following example to help you get started writing your own Loss of Home action plan.

Loss of Home Action Plan

Goal: Be able to recover my home after any event.

Step	Who	Action	Resources Needed
1	Anyone	Activate the loss of home action plan.	
2	Anyone	Obtain medical help for any family member (human or pet) who is hurt	▪ Contact details for medical services
3	Anyone	Assess the damage with officials for structural and internal damage (see Loss of Household Goods); determine damage to vehicles	▪ Camera for pictures of loss
4	Anyone	Contact insurance company	▪ Contact information for home (structure) insurance
5	Anyone	Secure home from further damage	▪ Tool Kit and materials
6	Anyone	Organize temporary housing if needed; be sure to secure home before leaving if possible	▪ Red Cross contact information if needed (and possibly FEMA) ▪ Contact details for family or friends who can provide assistance ▪ Various options should you be unable to return home for a few days, a week, two weeks, etc.

7	Anyone	Notification of your situation	▪ Communication Plan
			  ○ Work/School
			  ○ Family
			  ○ Friends
			  ○ Vendors (newspapers, mail, lawn, babysitter, alarm company, etc.)

8	Anyone	Options for daily routines if out of home for more than a few days	List of daily routines and deliveries
8	Anyone	Activate other checklists, if needed	Communications Plan Evacuation Plan I Evacuation Plan II Shelter in Place Loss of Utilities Loss of Adult Member Loss of Child Member Loss of Pet Loss of Household Goods Loss of Transportation Loss of Critical Records Identity Theft Loss of Job/Income

Your turn

Now it's your turn to write your plan. You may prefer to write your plan in more than one phase. You may decide that you will seek assistance from the Red Cross for the first two days, and then move to phase two, which involves temporary accommodation with a relative. If you are forced to be out of your home for, say, more than two weeks, you will probably need to include a third phase, for the longer term. In any case, think about what would work best for you and your entire family. You may want to contact other family members to determine whether they would be able to provide temporary accommodation at their home if something were to happen. Be assured, adjusting to living at a different location, even if it is only for a few days, is a whole lot easier if you have a pre-determined plan.

In putting together this plan, it will quickly become clear that you need some of the other parts of an emergency plan to make this recovery possible. For example, if you find you are suddenly without a home, you need a communications plan to notify friends, family, and co-workers about what has happened, and your immediate plans. Additionally, those vendors who supply services to your home (newspaper, mail delivery, gas or electric, lawn, pool, etc.) may not be required while you are absent from your home and therefore need to be notified. Depending on what has occurred, you may have needed to invoke one of the evacuation plans you made. If you didn't have an evacuation plan, you might not have survived! As you proceed to complete the remaining plans, you will see how some of them tie into each other.

Alternate benefit

When you decide you are going to move someplace else, you need to think about the impact on your day-to-day activities. It may change the time you need to get up in the morning to get to work or school, and learning the location of items in the aisles of a new grocery store can be taxing. You end up with new neighbors, and your mail is delivered at a different time.

You can use this type of plan to see what impacts you when you are no longer in your current home. This may help you to make decisions when looking for a new place to live – regardless of whether you own or rent. This may help you decide whether to stay in your current neighborhood or help you to feel comfortable about checking out other areas.

This disaster is very common, in fact despite the news headlines, it is more common than the impact of terrorist attacks. In 2006, the American Red Cross "responded to more than 74,000 disasters in communities across the United States, 93% of which were fire related." You should seriously think about doing this type of action plan!

The next action plan ties directly in to the loss of your home. The loss of a home generally includes the loss of household goods, so you need to have a plan to replace some or all of your possessions.

13

Loss of Household Goods Action Plan

Riches do not exhilarate us so much with their possession as they torment us with their loss.
EPICURUS

How many times have you seen the following scene on television: someone is standing on a cement slab where their house used to be, telling you that at least everyone got out okay before the fire destroyed everything they owned? Then they always talk about the loss of irreplaceable photos.

With this plan, when I ask you to focus on losing your household goods, I mean anything – and everything – in your home. This includes jewelry, electronic equipment, clothes, furniture, drapes, books, art works, linen, crockery, cutlery, and glassware, in addition to memorabilia such as family photos, etc. It also includes everything you have in your attic, basement, storage shed, and garage (other than your vehicles, which are covered in Chapter 14), together with your landscaping, pool equipment and outdoor furniture.

As with the loss of your home, you may experience anything from a partial loss to a total loss of household goods.

Examples

Some examples of events which may lead to either a partial or total loss of household goods include:

- Thieves break in while you're out and steal your PC, jewelry, digital camera, television, and your passport.
- Your house burns to the ground and everything is destroyed.
- A hurricane causes your roof to collapse, causing major damage to the second floor and all the furniture and contents there, together with some water damage to the first floor and its contents.

Questions to ask

You need to consider the following when completing your plan for loss of household goods:

- Are there any (working) warning systems for this type of emergency?
- How quickly do you want to be able to compile a complete list of everything in your home to submit to your insurance agent for reimbursement?
- What is your insurance deductible you must pay before you can be reimbursed?
- Is your insurance set up to replace these items at today's cost?
- Do you know how to contact and submit a report to your insurance company should you lose some or all of your household goods?
- How long after you submit a claim do you receive a reimbursement check?
- Does your insurance include any special coverage for any particular household goods?
- Can you easily access or replace critical documents, including those

which prove your identity if they are destroyed in the disaster?

- Can you identify critical items that are needed by each family member to survive for 1-3 days?
- Do you have custody of any family heirlooms or irreplaceable items?
- Do you have any items in your home belonging to your employer (e.g., laptop, printer, phone or other equipment, security ID, disks and/or data, etc.)
- Do you run a business out of your home?

Apply it

There are two things you need to make this plan work.

First, you need a complete and current inventory of everything you own. You need to be able to submit a comprehensive list to your insurance company for reimbursement. Although this sounds like a lot of work, it is actually not too bad.

Second, you need to ensure you have adequate insurance coverage. Not only should you have an adequate level of coverage in terms of dollar value to replace all your possessions, but you need to check on the terms and conditions of your insurance coverage. Most common home insurance policies only protect against fire, theft, lightning, and explosions. If you lose your household goods through some other event, you may find you are not covered. Further, if your loss is of lesser value than your deductible, you may be forced to replace your lost items out of your own pocket.

For those of you who rent, insurance against the loss of your household goods is *your* responsibility. The owner of your rental unit is responsible for insurance covering the structure, but this *does not* cover your possessions.

Sample

Review the following sample, and then get ready to write your Loss of Household Goods action plan.

Loss of Household Goods Action Plan

Goal: Be able to identify, compile a complete list, and submit a record to authorities as well as request for reimbursement to my insurance carrier of all goods lost within 3 business days of the event.

Step	Who	Action	Resources Needed
1	Anyone	Activate loss of household goods action plan.	
2	Anyone	Assess the total damage with authorities by identifying what was lost	▪ Full inventory of household goods ▪ Critical Records (backup)
3	Anyone	Obtain a police report	▪ Police report (need multiple copies)
4	Anyone	Contact your insurance carrier covering your household goods	▪ Contact information for insurance carrier including policy number and coverage ▪ Full inventory of household goods
5	Anyone	Submit paperwork to request reimbursement for lost items	▪ List of all goods lost or damaged ▪ Copy of Police Report ▪ Pictures of items lost or damaged, if available
6	Anyone	Activate other checklists, if needed	Communications Plan — Evacuation Plan I Evacuation Plan II — Shelter in Place Loss of Utilities — Loss of Adult Member Loss of Child Member — Loss of Pet Loss of Home — Loss of Transportation Loss of Critical Records — Identity Theft Loss of Job/Income

Your turn

As with the plan for the loss of your home, this one requires that you understand the coverage you have purchased from your insurance provider. Following Katrina, many home owners found out they were *not* covered, even though they had hurricane insurance, because the insurance companies said the damage was caused by the flooding when the levees broke – not by the hurricane itself. Be warned! Make sure you understand your coverage! And, if you are renting, the landlord's structure insurance does <u>not</u> cover your possessions if they are damaged or destroyed.

If you call your insurance agent about your coverage, you might also want to ask them about the process involved in submitting a claim, and how long it takes before you get a reimbursement check. It doesn't hurt to be informed.

Remember, the actual creation or collection of any resources you require, such as a complete household inventory, copies of critical documentation, backup photos, etc. is addressed in Phase 3 – *Collecting*. At this point, you should simply note them in your plan, and then move on to the next chapter.

Alternate benefit

Doing a complete inventory of your household goods can help you to better identify what type of, and how much, insurance you really need. Statistics show 64% of all homeowners are *under-insured* by an average of 27%. This means that if your household goods are currently valued at $100,000, there is a two in three chance you are underinsured by $27,000 (maybe less, but maybe a lot more, too). I don't know about you, but I can't afford to let $27,000 go up in flames! And this doesn't even take into account all the renters who are not insured at all. If you are renting, and your possessions are valued at $50,000 total, can you afford to kiss that kind of money goodbye?

Use this activity not only to make sure you are not *under*-insured, but also to ensure you are not *over*-insured, and paying too much to your insurance company. Remember, your inventory changes from year to year as your life changes with the purchase of new items and a purge of those that are no longer required, and so should your insurance coverage.

Another benefit to having a good inventory comes into play when you donate items to your favorite charity. If you have maintained an inventory year-over-year, you know the purchase price of the item(s) and when they were purchased. This will help you better estimate the value for your tax returns.

Basically, making a plan to cover a situation where you lose some or all of your household goods ensures you can make the transition to a temporary situation, and then on to recovery, easily. Ironically, without good documentation, it will be easier to collect reimbursement if you lose *everything* and not just some items. Why? If your home burns to the ground, you will get a check for the amount of your insurance policy. If you only lose *some* items, you may need to submit proof of ownership of those items, and if you're unable to provide proof, you may find it difficult to obtain reimbursement. Put yourself in their place. Would you readily pay out for something just because someone *said* they lost it, or would you want proof of ownership first?

The next chapter addresses the loss of your transportation. Whether you own a car or use public transportation, you need to come up with a plan to cover a scenario whereby you suddenly find yourself unable to get to work, school, or your normal activities by your usual means.

14

Loss of Transportation Action Plan

The shortest distance between two
points is under construction.
NOELIE ALITO

Whether we drive a car or use public transportation, each of us could find ourselves disoriented and severely disadvantaged were we to lose access to our usual means of transportation.

As with the loss of utilities, you need to look at this action plan with a view to a loss that may extend over a long period of time – not just an hour or a day.

Examples

Examples of potential situations that are addressed in this type of action plan include:

- Your house and all your vehicles, which are housed in the attached garage, are destroyed by a natural disaster or a house fire.

- You use public transportation to travel to and from work. You hear on the news that there is going to be a transportation workers' strike beginning tomorrow, and estimates are that the strike is going to last for quite a while.

- You turn 80, and the state revokes your driver's license.

- You're involved in a car accident. Fortunately, nobody is hurt, but the car is extensively damaged. Your insurance doesn't cover the cost of a rental car, and you can't afford to pay for one while yours is being repaired.

- A major snow storm causes widespread damage and dumps 30 inches of snow in your area. Authorities advise that nobody will be able to drive for at least the next three days while workers clear tree limbs and electrical wires from the roads.

- You have a medical condition which prohibits you from driving a car.

- The bridge that you use to get from your home to the center of town on the other side of the river is washed out by a flood, leaving you stuck at home until an alternative river crossing is built.

- You travel extensively for business, generally flying to various locations throughout the country. The prominent airline you always fly with is teetering on the brink of closing its doors.

Questions to ask

Our lives depend on transportation. No matter if you drive your own car or utilize a public system, we all need a ride someplace. And quite apart from our own mobility, we have come to take deliveries of vital supplies for granted. Think about the following issues as you begin to write your Loss of Transportation plan:

- Are there any (working) warning systems for this type of emergency?

- If I lose my normal mode of transportation, what are the available alternatives for me (and other family members) to get to work or school?

- What is my company's policy on working from home, and can I feasibly do my job from home?

- How long would my boss allow me to work from home if I was unable to get to work?

- If I was *not* able to work from home, how long would it be okay for me to not go in to work?

- If I was *not* able to work from home, how long would it be before the company began to dock my pay for lost days?

- Does my company have a policy which applies to this situation? If so, what is the policy?

- Could I be fired if I could not get in to work?

- Is there a point at which the cost of using my current mode of transportation becomes too expensive, and I need to find alternatives? For example, if the cost of gasoline reached $5.50 a gallon, would I need to look for alternatives, like car-pooling?

- Does the loss of transportation impact anyone in my family attending school? If so, what are the alternatives?

- Am I or my family at risk from a strike or a transportation system going out of business at a minutes notice, even if it only means our commute will take longer because there will be more cars on the road?

- If I suffered a blowout on the way home, would my spare tire be ready to use, along with the tools necessary to change the wheel?

Apply it

At the time of writing this book, the price of gas had more than doubled in the last few years. Many of us may end up being unable to drive our cars because we cannot afford the gas.

No matter the reason, think about the loss of your usual mode of transportation, and how it would impact your life. Think about what adjustments might be needed, and be sure to explore alternatives.

Sample

Everyone loves their cars, none more so than Americans, but you need to have an alternative plan, just in case. Use the following example to help you structure your plan, being sure to address *your* family's particular situation and needs.

Loss of Transportation Action Plan

Goal: Be able get to work/school/daily activities without being penalized should I lose my primary mode of transportation.

Step	Who	Action	Resources Needed
1	Anyone	Activate the loss of transportation action plan.	
2	Anyone	Contact car insurance carrier, if appropriate	• Contact information for insurance carrier including policy number and coverage • Contact information for auto club, if appropriate
3	Anyone	Contact vendors to fix car, if appropriate and determine length of time to fix	• Vendor names and numbers (provided by insurance carrier or family and friends)
4	Anyone	Arrange alternate options for work/school and/or find alternate transportation (rental car, car pooling, walking, riding bikes, public transportation, etc.)	• Company/school policy • Car insurance coverage (for rental car) • Public transportation contact number
5	Anyone	Determine changes to weekly routine based on changes in transportation	
6	Anyone	Activate other checklists, if needed	Communications Plan — Evacuation Plan I Evacuation Plan II — Shelter in Place Loss of Utilities — Loss of Adult Member Loss of Child Member — Loss of Pet Loss of Home — Identity Theft Loss of Household Goods — Loss of Job/Income Loss of Critical Records

Your turn

When you are doing your Loss *of Transportation Action Plan*, I recommend you contact your automobile insurance provider to ensure you understand your coverage. Ask them how, and how quickly, they would determine if your car is totaled after an accident. Find out if, and how quickly, you would get a rental car *(a)* if your car was damaged but repairable and *(b)* if it was totaled and you had to purchase a replacement. Those of you who use public transportation need to determine what you would do if it were unavailable for a period of time. Could you walk, get a lift with someone who drives a car, or maybe ride a bike?

Once you have the facts, you can then write a well-informed plan of action. And remember, if your car was damaged or destroyed in a road accident, the adult(s) in the family may not have survived. This information then becomes critical for those surviving family members who are trying to pick up the pieces.

Alternate benefit

As with your loss of household goods plan, checking with your insurance carrier in the course of reviewing this type of plan ensures that you are not *under*-insured (or *over*-insured) for all vehicles you own. Further, writing this type of plan may encourage you to explore alternate transportation options. You may find that riding a bike gives you more control, while providing you with daily exercise and generating a large saving on gas.

Perhaps you're thinking about starting a family, in which case one adult member is going to quit work and stay at home. Would one car suffice? Could alternate transportation fill in the gaps? If you know that reliable alternative transportation is available, selling one car to cut costs just might be an option.

If transportation plays an important part in your life, you should make sure you have an alternate plan you can immediately put into action should you lose your normal means of transportation. You don't want to be left stranded, and you don't want to be scrambling around at the last minute trying to get to work and trying to get the kids to school at the same time.

Now, you are going to think about what you would do if you lost your critical records. You may already have touched on this topic when you were looking at the loss of household goods, but now you are going to define what exactly constitutes critical records, identify where the originals are located, and determine whether you have a backup copy.

15

Loss of Critical Records Action Plan

Ninety-nine percent of the failures come from people who have the habit of making excuses.
GEORGE WASHINGTON

This is a different kind of loss than those that we have covered thus far. Everybody possesses a range of critical documents. Some are used every day, while others are used infrequently.

Some examples of critical documents include Wills, Powers of Attorney (both financial and medical), tax returns, financial records, irreplaceable family records (like photos), licenses, passports, insurance policies, etc. The loss of any one of these documents by themselves may not be a huge deal, however the loss of several or all of these documents, most likely in conjunction with other losses, such as the loss of your home due to a natural disaster, creates a much more critical situation.

For the purposes of this plan, you need to consider all documents that prove your identity, provide legal direction or guidance, confirm insurance coverage, confirm your financial status (what you owe, and/or what is due to you), and any other records that prove or confirm your status. You may want to include any personal documents or photographs that you consider irreplaceable should a disaster strike.

Examples

The following are example of scenarios that would require you to use this action plan:

- You are traveling overseas and lose your passport.

- A tornado batters your area, and afterwards you are unable to locate your wallet, which contains your license, medical insurance cards and credit cards.

- Your father has died, and you need to send a copy of his Death Certificate to the life insurance company before they will release a check, but you can't find the document.

- You are mugged, and your wallet, which contains your license, all your credit cards, your debit card, your social security card, and your employer's (building) access ID is stolen.

- Your dear friend suffers a heart attack, but you can't find the Living Will and Medical Power of Attorney you signed so that you could act on their behalf.

- All the photos of your late grandparents and parents are lost when a fire damages your home.

Questions to ask

Use the following questions to help you think about the steps you want to include in this plan:

- Are there any (working) warning systems for this type of emergency?

- What documents do I consider critical in relation to each adult, child and pet in the family?

- What are the critical documents I need to prove my financial status (what you owe, what is owed to you, tax returns, bank records, car title, deed to home, etc.)?

- What are the critical documents needed for insurance issues (life, long-term care, car, house, special insurances)?

- What are the critical documents issued by state/local government departments (birth certificate, license, state ID, car plates or license tag, marriage certificate, divorce decree, death certificate, drug program cards, etc.)?

- What are the critical documents issued by the federal government (social security card, passport, visas, Medicare/Medicaid cards, welfare records, etc.)?

- What are the critical documents issued by my employer (ID badge, parking sticker, benefits documentation such as health insurance cards, etc.)?

- What are the critical personal documents that belong to members of my family (family photos, citizenship papers, special awards, diplomas/degrees, etc.)?

- Are there any other critical documents?

Apply it

The term *critical documents* mean different things to different people. Most of us would agree that certain critical documents provide proof of identity. Examples would be your license, passport, or social security card. Other critical documents provide legal and financial direction such as a Will, tax returns, bank statements, etc. But don't forget the personal critical documents, which can include irreplaceable family photos and historical family documents.

First, you need to identify which documents are critical to you and your family, so when documents enter your home, you can immediately tag them as critical if necessary.

Second, if you identify a document as critical, you need to have a backup copy which is stored in a safe, yet accessible, location. No matter the circumstance, within reason, you should be able to access every critical document you need. Don't forget, the original is often stored with your attorney, accountant, state agency, federal agency, etc. You are simply looking at making a backup copy for convenient access in the event your primary copy is lost or destroyed.

Finally, you need to identify how quickly you want to be able to access either the original or the backup, should it become necessary. You may decide you need to be able to retrieve certain documents immediately, while others may take a back seat and be able to be retrieved later. For example, you should replace your driver's license within a few days if you lose it, so you need quick access to other documents that provide proof of ID, but if your tax returns from previous years are lost or damaged, there isn't the same degree of urgency.

Some of you may already have part of this action plan in place simply by virtue of having a safe deposit box, which is an excellent place to store those critical documents. However having such a box is only the first step. Someone else needs to know the box exists, be authorized to access it, and know where the key (and a spare) is located. If you already have a safe deposit box and a backup person who can access it, this is a very significant part of your emergency plan, and the rest is relatively easy. Good for you, taking this type of precaution for your family.

Sample

Some critical documents will be needed immediately following a disaster, while others may be retrieved at a later point. Be sure to have an action plan to retrieve copies, and be sure to identify which ones you will need first. The steps in the following example may apply to your particular situation, but you should feel free to add or substitute any other steps you feel are necessary.

Loss of Critical Records Action Plan

Goal: Be able to retrieve my critical documents when needed after they are lost or damaged.

Step	Who	Action	Resources Needed
1	Anyone	Activate the loss of critical records action plan.	
2	Anyone	Determine which document(s) you need and in which order	• List of critical documents and where backup copy is stored • If needed, identify who will retrieve each document
3	Anyone	Replace the backup copy with official/original copy	• Knowledge of timeline and agency/company to replace lost or damaged document
4	Anyone	Activate other checklists, if needed	Communications Plan, Evacuation Plan I, Evacuation Plan II, Shelter in Place, Loss of Utilities, Loss of Adult Member, Loss of Child Member, Loss of Pet, Loss of Home, Loss of Transportation, Loss of Household Goods, Identity Theft, Loss of Job/Income

Your turn

The approach you take will depend on the situation surrounding the loss of the critical document(s). You may want to design your action plan based on the assumption that *all* your documents have been lost. Your plan then lays out the logical order of retrieval of the copies.

If only *one* document is lost, then you simply follow the steps identified in your plan for that document.

Alternate benefit

By knowing which of your documents are critical, you can easily set up a file-purging process to remove documents that it is no longer legally necessary to retain. For example, you need to keep seven years' worth of tax returns. By knowing where the original is stored and where you backup copy is stored, you can perform regular reviews and remove the copies that are no longer required. Conducting an annual review keeps you on top of replacing soon to expire documents like licenses and passports *before* they expire – especially when you are required to initiate the replacement!

If you want to be able to retrieve critical documents, you need to know where the original is stored, where the backup copy is stored, how to get your hands on a copy, and how long the retrieval is likely to take. You also need to identify any security issues, such as who needs, and who has, access. This becomes very important if you are unable to retrieve these documents yourself.

A close relation to loss of critical documents is identity theft. In the next chapter, you will write out a plan of action should you encounter the loss of your identity for any reason. Don't be fooled - this is a common and increasingly prevalent crime today, all over the world.

16

Identity Theft Action Plan

If we don't act now to safeguard our privacy, we could all become victims of identity theft.
BILL NELSON

n today's fast-paced online world, identity theft is rapidly reaching epidemic proportions. The ease and speed with which criminals can steal your identity is frightening.

Loss of your identity can generate numerous problems, and totally disrupt your life. It is therefore an important part of your emergency plan.

Examples

Identity theft occurs when someone adopts your identity without your permission. Some examples of how this can happen include:

- Someone steals checks from your house or mailbox, and uses those checks to purchase goods and services for themselves.

- Someone intercepts your new credit card in the mail, and starts using it to make major purchases.

- You are attacked outside a store and your wallet, which contains all your credit cards and identification, is stolen.

- A hacker accesses your local government records online, and assumes your name, address, and social security number.

- Your doctor's office uses your social security number as your 'patient' number. A group of files, including yours, is stolen from the office.

- A vendor you (maybe no longer) use throws out old paper records *without* shredding them, and your personal information is now available to anyone who happens upon these papers (this can happen at *your* home if you don't shred all documents that you throw out which include your personal information!).

Questions to ask

The more detail you provide with this action plan, the faster you can complete your tasks. Use these questions to add detail to this action plan:

- Are there any (working) warning systems for this type of emergency?

- What should I do immediately if I discover I am a victim of identity theft?

- What is the process to file a police report regarding identify theft? Is there a special number to call, or should I simply call 911?

- Do I have access to any of the identity theft resolution companies (who can provide a personal advocate to walk you through the process)?

- Does my employer provide any identity theft resolution benefits?

- Does my bank or credit union offer any services or assistance to help with identity theft?

- Does my homeowner's insurance cover any expenses or provide assistance (free or for a fee) associated with identify theft?

- Have I collected as much detail as possible about the theft so I can report it to the police? For example, do I have a complete list of all the items stolen? Can I provide all account numbers, names and contact numbers for all credit cards, debit card information, license number, check information, paper files, computer files, etc.

- Are there any security issues associated with this loss? Think of items such as stolen keys or specific access information. Examples might be work-related ID badges, keys to secured work areas, home keys, car keys, lists of friends' telephone numbers and addresses, etc.

- Do I know how to report the identity theft to the three credit bureaus?

- Do I know how to report the theft of work-related items to my company?

- How quickly can a case of identity theft be resolved?

- Do I want to file a complaint with the Federal Trade Commission (FTC)?

Apply it

The tasks you include in this action plan are critical to your chances of success in responding to identity theft. I can assure you from personal experience, the longer it goes on without your knowledge, the longer it takes to clean it up. You need to make sure you have included all the necessary steps, and have easy access to this action plan.

Keep in mind that companies are required by law to notify you when their records have allowed your identity to be compromised in any way. You should receive a letter from the vendor explaining when the incident occurred, and a description of what was taken. From there, you need to take appropriate steps. An example of this occurred when a laptop computer containing personal details of 26 million military personnel was stolen. The government was required to notify all those people whose identities had been compromised.

Sample

May you never encounter this type of loss, but just in case you do, you can use the following example to help you set up your plan.

Identity Theft Action Plan

Goal: Be able to quickly and efficiently report identity theft as soon I realize it has occurred.

Step	Who	Action	Resources Needed
1	Anyone	Activate the identity theft action plan.	
2	Anyone	Contact the fraud department of <u>one</u> of the three consumer reporting companies. Place a <u>fraud alert</u> on your account. NOTE: This allows you to immediately receive a FREE credit report.	**Equifax:** 1-800-525-6285; www.equifax.com; P.O. Box 740241, Atlanta, GA 30374-0241 **Experian:** 1-888-EXPERIAN (397-3742); www.experian.com; P.O. Box 9532, Allen, TX 75013 **TransUnion:** 1-800-680-7289; www.transunion.com; Fraud Victim Assistance Division, P.O. Box 6790, Fullerton, CA 92834-679
3	Anyone	Close any of your existing accounts you feel have been tampered with; close any account opened by someone other than you	
4	Anyone	File a complaint with the FTC (by telephone, in writing, or online)	**1-877-IDTHEFT** (438-4338) Identity Theft Clearinghouse Federal Trade Commission 600 Pennsylvania Ave., NW, Washington, DC 20580 http://www.ftc.gov/
5	Anyone	File a report with the police department (in the locality where the theft took place)	▪ Copy of your FTC complaint
6	Anyone	Call vendors and replace stolen items	▪ Communication List for all vendors with telephone numbers, e-mail, and/or addresses ▪ Copies of FTC Complaint ▪ Copies of the Police report
7	Anyone	Activate other checklists, if needed	Communications Plan — Evacuation Plan I Home Evacuation II — Shelter in Place Loss of Utilities — Loss of Adult Member Loss of Child Member — Loss of Pet Loss of Home — Loss of Transportation Loss of Household Goods — Loss of Job/Income Loss of Critical Records

Your turn

Now it's your turn to set up your Identity Theft action plan. Remember, enter resource information is you have it readily available, or wait for the next section – *Collecting*.

Alternate benefit

Keeping track of your personal information by reviewing your credit report at least once a year allows you to ensure you are in healthy financial shape if you decide to purchase a home or car, or apply for additional credit. You are permitted by law to obtain a *free* copy of your credit *report* once a year to check for irregularities. You can get this copy by simply calling or going online to any one of the three credit bureaus.

You must *pay* for a copy of your credit *score*.

Remain vigilant at all times. As part of your family emergency plan, I have provided a 12-month calendar to help keep your plan up to date. You can be sure that checking your credit report is included.

Losing your identity could be devastating, and so could losing your job, particularly if it is unexpected. In the next chapter, you are going to come up with a plan of action should you ever lose your job.

Elizabeth M. Owen

17

Loss of Job/Income Action Plan

Recession is when a neighbor loses his job.
Depression is when you lose yours.
HARRY S. TRUMAN

I t used to be rare to see someone laid off from a job. Now, we see it every-day, in communities everywhere. Even the biggest corporations no longer offer a secure future or a job for life. It also used to be a rare occurrence when an already-retired person lost their health insurance originally paid by their company. In today's world, taking back or scaling down this already-earned benefit is on the rise. The added cost to keep this benefit is passed on to the retiree who must pay it or lose their coverage.

This action plan also covers situations where you suddenly incur additional unexpected expenses which exceed your regular income. For those of you who are retired, there may come a time when your corporation pulls your health insurance coverage. You may be under the impression your health insurance is secure for life, but some companies are no longer including retired employees in their schemes due to rising costs. In a slightly better scenario, retirees may have to start paying part of their health insurance premium because their former employer puts a cap on their contribution. Either way, increased expenses of this nature can throw your budget into a tailspin.

123

Even if you haven't experienced the loss of a job or an unexpected increase in expenses yet, you need to be both realistic and prepared.

Examples

There are many ways of losing your job/income. Here are a few examples:

- Your employer's building burns to the ground, and they have no Disaster Recovery and Continuity Plan. The insurance is insufficient to cover the costs of rebuilding, so they are forced to close their doors. You lose your job on the spot, including all benefits and pay.

- The company you work for is moving to another state. You are offered a job there, but you don't want to move, so you decline the offer. You have just two months before you are out of a job. There will be a severance package, but it's based on years of service, and you have only been with them for three years.

- Your employer is forced to shut down for at least 90 days for repairs following a natural disaster. The owner plans to re-open, and is pretty sure there will be a job for you, but until then, you have no job, and no benefits to tide you over.

- You are a stay-at-home parent, and your spouse, who brings in all of your family's income, dies in a car accident.

- The major employer in your area shuts down its facility and lays off all its employees. These people represent 80% of your employer's customers. You figure you might have 1-3 months at best before your company starts to feel this loss and you get laid off.

- You retired three years ago and your former employer has continued to pay the majority of your health insurance premiums. Now they advise you that because of rising health costs, they can no longer continue to contribute. Your monthly payment rises from $50 to $475.

- Your position is outsourced.

- Your company is bought out and you are made redundant.

- You take an offer of early retirement so you can be sure to lock in at least some benefits.

- You have been working as a consultant when the funding for your project is pulled.

- Your entire department is eliminated as part of a cost-cutting exercise.

Questions to ask

You need to focus on the loss of your job and/or benefits (which may mean increased expenses). Review this list based on your current situation:

- Are there any (working) warning systems for this type of emergency?

- Do I have an up-to-date copy of my resume I can easily put my hands on if I were to lose my job?

- Who would I use for references?

- Do I have examples of work I have completed to use when job hunting? NOTE: This assumes you are allowed to have copies of your work.

- Where would I look for another job? For example, would I just use the newspapers, or would I need a computer to check online sources? For all sources, be sure to include your ability to access them.

- Do I have a network of friends, or colleagues in my field of expertise (maybe with competitors, customers or suppliers) who I could contact?

- By losing my job, do I have other options for accessing the internet to search for a new job?

- Do I know which headhunters focus on my line of work?

- If I were to lose my job, what other sources of income are there and can my family survive solely on these alternative sources?

- What alternative sources of funds are available? Examples include savings, CDs, money market accounts, liquid assets, cars, boats, properties, etc.

- Do I know how much my monthly expenses are?

- If I were to be laid off, does my company offer a severance package? If so, what does it include?

- If my company needed to close temporarily (say 30-90 days) for any reason, would I be able to hold out, or would I need another job immediately? Could I collect unemployment (eligibility is usually based on your recent work history)?

- Would I consider moving to another city for a job? Would my family also move, or would I have to commute?

- Are there any items I could cut out of my monthly expenses were I to lose my job or had to begin paying for benefits?

- Which of my benefits are critical, and which ones are in the *nice to have* category? Do I have any options for the critical benefits?

Apply it

This particular loss scenario can really hit the pocketbook hard. Although financial coaches always say to have 3-6 months salary in the bank as a *minimum*, that's not always possible. You need to take a hard look at what you have, prioritize your benefits, and know where you can cut expenses if needed.

Sample

In today's world, this type of loss is a very real possibility. Review the following example and then begin writing your plan. You should have a plan for everyone in the family who has a job.

Loss of Job/Income Action Plan

Goal: Be able to immediately begin searching for an income source should I lose my primary source or if I should be hit with additional, unexpected expenses.

Step	Who	Action	Resources Needed
1	Anyone	Activate the loss of job/income action plan.	
2	Anyone	Retrieve my resume, if applicable	• Up-to-date, accessible copy (electronic and/or paper) of my resume • Up-to-date list of references
3	Anyone	Solicit contacts for open positions	• Up-to-date network contacts in field • Up-to-date network contacts from previous jobs/college • Up-to-date network contacts — family/friends • List of vendors
4	Anyone	Complete financial impact/changes needed; determine point where you are in trouble with paying bills	• List of what is owed/to whom • List of optional (nice to have) expenses • Other sources of income
5	Anyone	File with State for unemployment, if appropriate	• Contact information for State unemployment • Records from employer required for filing
7	Anyone	Activate other checklists, if needed	Communications Plan Evacuation Plan I Evacuation Plan II Shelter in Place Loss of Utilities Loss of Adult Member Loss of Child Member Loss of Pet Loss of Home Loss of Transportation Loss of Household Goods Identity Theft Loss of Critical Records

Your turn

Remember, even if the company you work for is stable today, if they do not have their own Business Disaster Recovery & Continuity Plan, you are at risk. Without a corporate emergency plan, there is just one disaster between you collecting a paycheck with benefits and being unemployed. Before putting together your own action plan, you might want to check if your company does indeed have a plan, and If they don't, keep that thought in mind as you prepare yours. If you don't have a family emergency plan, your family could be impacted in the same way. Here today, gone tomorrow.

The best part about this action plan is that you may be able to do just *one* plan to cover all family members who currently hold jobs. Copies of each resume can be kept in one location, and resources for finding available jobs may be able to be shared. Each person will need to keep their own list of network contacts who might be able to offer assistance.

If you do not have a computer at home, or you want to protect yourself in case your computer is destroyed or stolen, it is recommended you keep at least one *paper* copy of your current resume (critical record?) and at least one electronic copy as a backup.

For those who are already retired, the loss of retiree benefits such as medical coverage is a concern, and a very real possibility. You need to be prepared, just in case, by being knowledgeable about your options. You may also need an up-to-date resume, should you need to go back to work.

Alternate benefit

Being prepared in case you lose your job requires you to always have your resume up to date. Another major reason to keep your resume current is to ensure that you are prepared should you come across a job that is perfectly suited for you. If you don't have your resume current, you may miss an opportunity to snag the job of your dreams.

This type of plan can also be used to check if your family can survive on one salary. Situations often arise whereby one adult member may want to leave the corporate environment to start their own business, work less hours, have a baby, etc. This type of plan allows you to take a realistic view of your position, and determine whether a reduction in total income is workable.

Basically, this type of plan is what I call Plan B. I have always had an idea in my head of what I would do were I to lose my job, because it helps you to land on your feet. If lots of people lose their job at the same time, it puts you 10 steps ahead of everyone else. You are immediately ready to go, while they're still trying to figure out how to get a copy of their resume. Jump to the front of the line by being prepared.

Congratulations! You have now completed your action plans. The work you have done has definitely put your household in a better position to cope and adjust should a disaster occur.

Are you now ready to finish this thing up? Let's move on to Phase 3 – *Collecting*.

PHASE 3

Collecting

Elizabeth M. Owen

I f you have reached this section of the book, I assume you have completed all your action plans. Just think how much more protected your family is now than they were before you started this activity!

Phase 3 is called *Collecting* for a very good reason. As the title implies, you now need to collect and assemble all the resources you identified as being critical to the success of each of your action plans but have not yet gathered. How well and how quickly you assemble these resources can make or break the effectiveness of your plans and how well your family is protected.

To buy or not to buy

You can choose how you pull together your resources. For example, some resources are going to be available in the form of pre-packaged kits. If you have the money and time is limited, you may elect to purchase a kit instead of putting one together yourself. Some resources however will require you to collect or assemble them yourself.

As you look through your lists, select the options which best suit your budget and available time. Don't rule out the option of a mixture of some pre-packaged resources and some that are personally compiled.

Your timeframe

The next decision you need to make has to do with just how fast you want to collect all your resources. Remember, the sooner they are all gathered together, the sooner your family is best protected.

Collecting all your resources immediately is, by far, your best option. Your family will be protected as quickly as possible.

Some people may decide they need a little time to collect all the resources they need, and might set a timeframe of three months (you can select a timeframe that works for you). This is the next best option, because while the collection of resources is not going to happen immediately, it is not an extended timeframe, and a completion date has been set. Understand though, that until all the resources are in place, your family remains vulnerable.

If you feel you are unable to adopt either of these approaches, you can use the 12-month calendar found in *Phase 4 – Testing and Maintaining*, to organize your resource-collection activities. Each month you can address the resources related to what is scheduled for that month. In terms of your family's protection, this approach provides the least amount of security, because you will be leaving your family exposed for up to 12 months while you gather your resources. You risk leaving your family unprepared should something happen during this period.

That said you are now ready to begin collecting your resources. The chapters in this section are divided into two categories, supplies and information, to make the task easier. You need to refer to your completed action plans to identify the resources you will need.

18

Survival Kits

It is not the strongest of the species that survives,
nor the most intelligent that survives.
It is the one that is the most adaptable to change.
CHARLES DARWIN

As mentioned previously, survival is the primary focus when confronted with a disaster. The first 72 hours are critical. Be aware that your local responders – fire, police, and medical – are going to give priority to those who are in greatest need, or those who they are able to reach. Only after they have attended to those people can they move on to assist less pressing cases, and those who have previously been out of reach.

It is recommended that every family be prepared to survive without assistance for a minimum of 72 hours, though after Hurricane Katrina devastated New Orleans, organizations like the American Red Cross began recommending that people consider being prepared to survive for up to two weeks if necessary. You need to decide on the appropriate timeframe for your family, based on your particular situation and likely risks.

Keep in mind though, assembling and maintaining survival kits should only take a few hours of your time each year.

Types of kits

There are several types of kits you need if you are to survive and recover from disasters. The most common ones include:

- **Water Kit** – water for each family member, including water for cooking and personal hygiene.

- **Food Kit** – food that is familiar to the family, yet can be easily stored.

- **First Aid Kit** – basic medical tools and supplies.

- **Personal Pack** – items for each family member such as toothbrushes, spare pairs of eyeglasses/contacts, medicines, sleepwear, cash or credit cards, etc. These personal items may be packaged as separate kits or combined with clothing and bedding kits.

- **Clothing and Bedding Kit** – at least one change of clothing for every family member, season-appropriate if you live in an area where the weather changes significantly, and temporary bedding.

- **Tools and Supplies** – basic tools and materials to enable temporary repairs to be made, or to help with the cleanup process.

- **Sanitary Items** – this includes bathroom-related items, disinfectant, etc.

- **Pet Kits** – for each pet, you need supplies of food, water and any medicines used, as well as contact information for the veterinarian, and identification details.

Over the next few pages, you will find a checklist for each of these kits. If you have identified any of them as a resource while completing Phase 2, feel free to copy the relevant checklist to help you put your kit together.

Each kit includes a suggested storage option. Some recommend an airtight, water-proof container, pre-packed so they can be moved easily, for example a plastic *box* with a snap-on lid large enough to hold all items, but not too heavy for anyone to pick up. Others, such as your change of clothing kit, can be stored in a suitcase or backpack. Be sure to review the Budget-wise options alternative as another option.

A recommended timeline for replenishing supplies is provided for each kit, where relevant, and checking these kits is part of the 12-month calendar in Phase 4 – *Testing and Maintaining*. If you feel you need to replenish or re-place any item more frequently, or add any additional items, you can simply amend the calendar accordingly.

If there are any special items or kits you identified while writing your action plans, this is the time to put them in place. These items or kits may be related to a specific medical condition of a family member, religious be-liefs, special food requirements, your particular geographical location, etc. When you get to the 12-month calendar, you will be reminded to include these customized kits wherever they best fit in with your annual maintenance activities.

When you get to Phase 4 – *Testing and Maintaining*, you will learn how to make sure these kits are always ready should you need them.

Let's get started with the common kits.

Water Kit

A water kit is critical for basic survival for every household. When put-ting together a water kit, keep the following in mind:

- Determine the length of time you want to be able to keep your family supplied with fresh water (a minimum of three days is recommended)
- Store one gallon of water per person per day (½ gallon for drinking and ½ gallon for food preparation and/or sanitation)
- Regularly replenish your supply
- Store your water in a portable container that is easy to pick up and carry in case you need to evacuate

- Include a two-week supply of water for each pet (one fluid ounce of water per two pounds of your pet/s weight per day)
- You should also include drinking cups, a pot for boiling (in case water becomes contaminated), regular bleach (for purification) and a drinking dish for each pet.

Time-wise options

To save time in preparing a water kit, purchase prepackaged water in wrapped cases, and either keep the bottles in the wrapped cases or transfer them to your own container.

Ensure that everyone knows where the water is stored (basement, garage, pantry, laundry room, etc.). Don't store the water near a furnace or other heating/cooling unit, and don't store the water near any chemicals or paints.

Budget-wise options

If bottled water is beyond your budget, or you simply don't think it is necessary, an economical alternative is to fill empty soda bottles with tap water. Make sure you clean the bottles thoroughly.

This option requires a little more attention in terms of maintenance, since you need to make sure the water remains as fresh and as clean as possible. You will need to replenish each bottle on a regular basis (maybe once a month). A variation is to clean and fill your first set of soda bottles, then whenever you finish another bottle, clean it out and fill it with fresh water from the tap and use it to replace one of the old bottles. It is a good idea to label each bottle with the date it was last replenished, so you always replace or replenish the oldest water. This ensures that your family's water kit is always ready to use.

Fill enough bottles to provide the amount of water you have decided you need to survive for your designated timeframe. Store the bottles in a portable container. This can be something as simple as a plastic grocery store bag (you may want to double-bag to avoid breakage). Ensure that all family members know where the water supply is stored. As with pre-packaged water, do not store your kit near heating/cooling units or near any chemicals or paints.

Here's an easy-to-use checklist to make sure you have enough fresh water stored for the designated timeframe.

Start by listing each family member on the left had side. Decide how many days you need to be self-sufficient and record the amount required, based on one gallon per day for each member. For example, if you want to be self-sufficient for up to five days, and you have four family members, you will need 20 gallons of water.

For pets, you may want to increase the timeframe to allow for the possibility of having them cared for at a shelter or by a relative, friend or neighbor for an extended period. It's your choice.

Water Kit

Rotation: Six-months (using pre-packaged); monthly (self-assembled)

Storage: Portable container; cool dark area; **not** near flammables/pesticides; designated location known and accessible to all family members

To purify water: Boil water, if possible

Otherwise, ¼ gallon of water + 2 drops of bleach if water is clear, or ¼ gallon of water + 4 drops of bleach if water is cloudy

---

Members:

- 5 days supply per member
- 1 gallon per day per member
- ½ gallon for drinking; ½ gallon for food preparation/hygiene

_____

_____

_____

_____

_____

_____

_____

_____

_____

_____

- Bleach
- Cups for drinking
- Dishes for pet
- Pot for boiling
- ☐ ___gallons
- ☐ ___gallons
- ☐ ___gallons
- ☐ ___gallons
- ☐ ___gallons
- ☐ ___gallons
- ☐ ___gallons
- ☐ ___gallons
- ☐ ___gallons
- ☐ ___gallons

TOTAL human requirements: _____

Pets:

- ___ days supply
- One fluid oz. per two pounds of pet weight per day

_____

_____

_____

- ☐ _____ water x ___ days _____
- ☐ _____ water x ___ days _____
- ☐ _____ water x ___ days _____

TOTAL pet requirements: _____

TOTAL WATER NEEDED: _____ **gal.**

Food Kit

Food is just as critical for your family members as water. Use the following guide to help you assemble a food kit:

- After deciding how long you need to survive without help, calculate and store the necessary amount of food for all family members
- Select foods which do not require refrigeration, are not difficult to prepare, do not increase thirst (are not too salty), and do not require a lot of water to cook
- Select lightweight foods (easier to carry in an evacuation)
- If possible, include foods that are familiar to your family (comfort foods)
- Consider ready-to-eat meats, canned fruits and vegetables, canned or boxed juices, low-sodium crackers, peanut butter, jelly, granola bars, trail mix, cookies, hard candy, instant coffee, tea, powdered milk, and cereals
- Store all food in portable containers (ready for evacuation)
- Include canned or dried pet food for pets
- Include the following items in your food kit: manual can opener, plastic wrap, tin foil, knives, forks, spoons, paper plates/cups, cooking pot/s, dish-washing soap, wet-wipes (to clean up after eating), plastic containers and storage bags.

Time-wise option

Purchase food that is specifically intended for your survival kit separate from your everyday food purchases. Every six months, replenish the existing kit with fresh supplies. Be sure to include the items needed to access, prepare and serve the food.

Budget-wise options

Instead of purchasing additional food specifically for an emergency, store some everyday items in a plastic grocery store bag and keep it in your pantry or somewhere else that makes sense. I call this an *integrated* food kit. If you need something from it for one of your regular meals, simply use it, and pick up a replacement the next time you go to the store. Ensure that every family member understands where this kit is stored, and understands that it is your survival supply.

Keep all your food and associated items in a portable, air-tight container. Ensure that all family members know where the kit is stored, and have access to it. As with your water kit, don't store your food kit near any heating/cooling units, paint, or chemicals.

Here's a checklist for your food kit. As with the water kit, list the names of all family members down the left hand side, and determine how many days' supply you need. Then list all your pets, and determine how many days' supply is appropriate for them.

Food Kit

Rotation: Six-month (if you have a separate food kit); on-going (if you integrated food with water kit)
Storage: Portable, air-tight container in a designated location; **not** near flammables/pesticides; known by all family members

Consider: ready-to-eat meats, canned fruits and vegetables, canned or boxed juices, low-sodium crackers, peanut butter, jelly, granola bars, trail mix, cookies, hard candy, instant coffee, tea, powdered milk, cereals

- Select days required
- No refrigeration required
- Little or no preparation

Members:

_____
_____
_____
_____
_____
_____
_____
_____
_____

Pets:

- ____ days supply
- Canned or dry

_____
_____
_____

- Familiar to family
- Doesn't increase thirst (limit salt)
- Requires little or no water
- Lightweight (for evacuation)

____ days supply
____ days supply
____ days supply
____ days supply
____ days supply
____ days supply
____ days supply
____ days supply
____ days supply

____ days supply
____ days supply
____ days supply

- ☐ Aluminum Foil
- ☐ Plastic wrap
- ☐ Heavy duty aluminum foil
- ☐ Can opener (manual)
- ☐ Pet feeding supplies/dishes

- ☐ Cooking/eating utensils
- ☐ Cooking pots/pans
- ☐ Paper plates/cups/utensils
- ☐ Cooking fuel
- ☐ Plastic containers/storage bags

First Aid Kit

Your first aid kit should include basic tools and supplies to enable you to administer first aid in the event that one or more family members sustain injuries. You can either assemble your own kit, or purchase a kit from one of several reputable vendors. Consider the following items for your kit:

- First aid book/instructions

- Cloth bandages (assorted sizes), adhesive bandages (assorted sizes), adhesive tape (assorted sizes), antibiotic ointment for dressing, hydrogen peroxide (to wash wounds), splint materials, and sterile dressing/gauze

- Medicines such as anti-diarrhea medicine, laxatives, antacids, anti-nausea tablets, aspirin, cough mixture or lozenges, vitamin supplements, syrup ipecac (to induce vomiting), pain killers (Acetaminophen) and smelling salts

- Lotions including calamine, sunscreen, insect repellant, hand sanitizer, skin lotions, and petroleum jelly/lubricant

- Tools such as tweezers, disposable latex gloves, scissors, safety pins (assorted), a pocket knife (Swiss Army style), cotton balls/swabs, premoistened towelettes, tissues, needle and thread, thermometer, eye wash cup and sterile water, surgical masks, and safety razor blades

- Store in a portable, air-tight container (for easy evacuation)

- Replenish supplies when they are depleted or when they reach their expiration date

Time-wise options

You can purchase pre-packaged kits from local suppliers or online. They are generally white with a large red cross, making them easily identifiable. If you don't want to purchase a pre-packaged kit, but still want to maintain a separate supply just for emergencies, purchase the supplies you require and place them in a portable, air-tight container, which becomes your emergency first-aid kit. Expiration dates are critical in relation to medicines. Be sure every family member knows where the kit is located and can access it if needed.

Budget-wise options

As with the food and water kits, you don't necessarily need to purchase medical supplies specifically for emergency purposes. You probably (indeed you should) have many of the items in your home already, and can therefore use an *integrated* medical kit. Simply store the emergency items in a bag or container in an appropriate location in your house. Make sure the container is portable, air-tight, and easy to lift, and that every family member knows where it is, and can access it if required. This way, you can still access it and use it as needed on a daily basis, but it is also ready for an immediate evacuation if required.

First Aid Kit

Rotation: Use **expiration dates, and replace any items used**
Storage: Portable, air-tight container; in a designated location known to all family members

Medicine:

☐ Hydrogen Peroxide (to wash wounds)	☐ Cough mixture or lozenges
☐ Anti-diarrhea medicine	☐ Vitamin supplements
☐ Laxatives	☐ Antibiotic ointment for dressing
☐ Antacids	☐ Smelling salts
☐ Anti-nausea tablets	☐ Pain killers (Acetaminophen)
☐ Aspirin	☐ Syrup ipecac (to induce vomiting)

Other:

☐ Tweezers	☐ Needle and thread
☐ Splint material	☐ Non-breakable thermometer
☐ Disposable latex gloves	☐ Eye wash cup and sterile water
☐ Scissors	☐ Surgical masks
☐ Safety pins (assorted)	☐ Safety razor blades
☐ Pocket knife (Swiss Army style)	☐ Elastic bandages (assorted)
☐ Adhesive bandages (assorted)	☐ Bandages (assorted)
☐ Sterile dressing/gauze	☐ Adhesive tape (assorted)
☐ First aid book	☐ Bar of soap
☐ Cotton balls/swaps	☐ Hand sanitizer
☐ Pre-moistened towelettes	☐ Skin lotions
☐ Tissues	☐ Calamine and sunscreen lotions
☐ Petroleum jelly/lubricant	☐ Insect repellent
☐ Scissors	☐ First Aid Book/Instructions
☐ _____	☐ _____
☐ _____	☐ _____
☐ _____	☐ _____
☐ _____	☐ _____
☐ _____	☐ _____
☐ _____	☐ _____

Personal Packs

This can be used in two different ways. First, it is truly a pack of personal items for each family member. In this sense, it is used in conjunction with your Clothing and Bedding Kit (see the next section) to make a complete pack for each family member.

Alternatively, it can be used on its own as a Personal Pack/Mini Clothing kit for anyone who feels that the Clothing and Bedding kit is unnecessary.

In the event of an immediate evacuation, such as a house fire, the personal pack should be easy to access and take with you, if the situation permits. Each family member should pack their own items. Think about how you want to use this pack, but consider including the following items:

- Basic toiletries (toothbrush, hairbrush/comb, shampoo, deodorant, razor, shaving cream, lip balm, makeup, etc.)
- Eyeglasses/contact lenses/supplies
- Complete set of house and car keys
- Cash
- Credit/debit card
- Medications for a minimum of three days (per person) or longer if you feel it is necessary
- Pet medications for a minimum of one week (for each pet) or longer if you feel it is necessary
- Hearing aid/battery
- Whistle
- Camera (disposable is fine) to record the damage if appropriate, along with a pad and a (sharpened) pencil (a pencil is recommended because pens may be damaged or may dry up)
- Other items, including: sunglasses, toys (to calm and settle children), and a cell phone with a fully-charged battery and/or a battery charger

- Change of underwear (including diapers for infants), sleepwear, and one change of clothes (specific to the climate/time of year) if you do not want to prepare a standard Clothing and Bedding kit

- If you choose not to prepare water and food kits, it is recommended that you store a limited supply of water and food (for example a bottle of water and breakfast bars or crackers) in your Personal Pack

Time-wise options

Purchase additional personal items and store them in backpacks. Depending on the disasters you identified in Chapter 2 as more likely to happen where you live, store the backpacks near the most logical exit from your house. You should also think about keeping an identical pack offsite, at a relative's, friend's or neighbor's house, or at work, just in case you are unable to get to the pack in your home.

Budget-wise options

When items such as deodorants or contact solution are nearly finished, replenish your everyday supply, and place the nearly-finished items in your Personal Pack. Again, this can be a backpack, which is easy to slip onto your back in the event of an evacuation, or it can be any other type of portable container. When you get your new glass prescription filled, put the old glasses in the bag. Sure, it means you won't be seeing perfectly if you need to use them, but you'll see much better than you would without any corrective lenses at all. The sleepwear and underwear can also be old clothing that has been replaced. Remember, you're packing for an emergency, not a vacation, and you're packing in case you are forced to evacuate your home and are unable to return for an unknown period.

You should store the personal packs in a closet by the main exit door, in your trunk, or at a remote location such as a relative's, friend's or neighbor's home. Consider this kit as a supplement to your Clothing and Bedding kit if one has been prepared.

Personal Packs

Rotation:	As used
Storage:	Grab-and-go pack (like a backpack); locate for easy access in the event of an evacuation

❑ Extra eyeglasses/contacts

❑ Toiletries (toothbrush, hair comb, shampoo, deodorant, razor, shaving cream, lip balm, makeup, etc.)

❑ Contact lens supplies

❑ Sunglasses

❑ Toys

❑ Entertainment/Books/Games

❑ Identification

❑ Communications Plan

❑ Complete set of keys

❑ Cash

❑ Credit/Debit Card/Checks

❑ Hearing aid/battery

❑ Cell phone

❑ Cell phone battery/charger

❑ Camera (to document destruction)

❑ Pad/Pencil

❑ Whistle

Medication/Prescriptions:

❑ _____

❑ _____

❑ _____

❑ _____

❑ _____

❑ _____

❑ _____

Include all human and pet members:

____ days supply

____ days supply

____ days supply

____ days supply

____ days supply

____ days supply

____ days supply

Other Items (clothes/water/food):

❑ _____

❑ _____

❑ _____

❑ _____

❑ _____

❑ _____

Clothing and Bedding Kit

Some of you may elect to prepare a full-blown Clothing and Bedding kit in addition to the Personal Pack. This type of kit is useful if you're required to evacuate your home and are not sure how long it will be before you are able to return. An ideal container for this kit is an old suitcase, maybe one without rolling wheels. When preparing your clothing and bedding kit, think about the following:

- Again, you're *not* packing for a vacation, you're packing clothes to wear while you sit in a shelter, clean up around your home, wait out a storm in a hotel room, etc., so think about packing old clothes you no longer wear
- At least one complete change of clothes per person, *appropriate* for the current season
- Sleepwear for each family member (I recommend children's favorite sleepwear, to help with comforting)
- Extra socks and underwear (thermal if appropriate) for each person
- Sturdy shoes/work boots for each person
- Rain gear for each person
- Hats and gloves for each person (either summer or winter as appropriate)
- Baby needs/elderly person needs
- Store in an easy-to-grab suitcase or portable container

For a bedding kit, think about the following if either your family or first responders need sleeping supplies:

- Blankets or sleeping bags for each person
- Pillows, if needed
- Pet bedding/carrying case

- Store in an easy-to-move, water-proof container
- Items found in a Personal Pack (if not packed separately)

Time-wise options

Pack two different suitcases, one with spring/summer clothes, and the second with fall/winter clothes. Keep both suitcases in the same area, but be sure they are clearly labeled so you can grab the correct one. Add other items to your kit as appropriate for your family's situation. One suitcase, packed with the entire family's clothing needs, makes things simple. If you have sleeping bags, store these with the suitcases, so they can be accessed and used.

Budget-wise options

Keep a set of clothing for each family member in one container. Be sure it is located in a readily accessible area, and all family members know where it is. One change of clothes (underwear and outer garments) for day and night is the minimum requirement. If you have extra bedding, be sure to pack it and leave it near the clothes container. Be sure everyone has solid shoes to wear. If you have old bedding material that you no longer use, you can store it with this kit.

Clothing and Bedding Kit

Rotation: As Used

Storage: Portable container/suitcase; located in a designated location known to all family members; should be season appropriate

Used in conjunction with the Personal Pack; May be needed by rescue workers (instead of, or in addition to, your family)

❑ Blankets or sleeping bag for each person

❑ One complete change of clothes for each person for the current season

❑ Extra socks

❑ Extra underwear

❑ Thermal underwear, if appropriate

❑ Pet carrying case

❑ Sturdy shoes/work boots for each person

❑ Rain gear for each person

❑ Hat and gloves for each person

❑ Pillows

❑ Baby needs, including diapers for three days

❑ Elderly person needs

❑ Sleepwear for each person

Tools and supplies

This kit is directed more at homeowners, so if you rent, you may not need this kit, however I recommend you review this section because some of the items would be beneficial to have on hand in the event of a disaster, no matter who owns the property.

There's every chance you will need to clean up and/or effect some running repairs around your home after any disaster. This includes cutting up fallen trees, patching holes in your roof, securing your home by fixing broken windows, etc. Depending on your particular situation, a Tools and Supplies kit could contain:

- Basic supplies such as a hammer, nails, screwdriver, wood, etc.
- Axe (for clean-up purposes, although you may want to store one in your attic in case flooding forces you to take refuge there and you need to escape through the roof)
- Waterproof tarps
- Flashlight and extra batteries
- Matches (stored in a plastic bag to keep dry)
- Fire extinguisher
- Shovel
- Work gloves
- Disposable dust masks

You should keep your Tools and Supplies kit in a portable plastic container and store it in an easily-accessible area such as your garage. It will probably be easier to retrieve this kit if it is in the garage rather than the basement.

Your Tools and Supplies kit should also include some basic sanitary items. You're going to need to go to the bathroom, and may not have access to a working toilet and sink. Plus, there is a strong possibility the water in your neighborhood may have become polluted. Think about including the following items in your Tools and Supplies kit to cater for these most basic of human needs:

- Medium sized plastic bucket with lid (for toilet)
- Plastic garbage bags and ties
- Household chlorine bleach (to purify water)
- Disinfectant
- Plastic and duct tape (to allow you to shelter-in-place in the event of a chemical release)
- Toilet paper
- Hand sanitizer

Store these additional items in a portable plastic container along with the rest of your Tools and Supplies kit.

Time-wise options

You may want to be a little selective in terms of which items you include, depending on where you live and the types of disasters which pose a risk to your family and property. If you rent, you might not need all of these items, and may decide that a flashlight, some matches and the sanitary items are all that is required.

You can purchase a pre-packaged tool kit with a hammer, screwdriver, etc., and you can also purchase a portable toilet with appropriate supplies. A flashlight which works simply by shaking (no batteries required) would be a useful addition to your kit.

Budget-wise options

If you already own many of the tools and other items listed (such as a flashlight), simply ensure they are gathered together in one area. Keep them in a portable container to make it easier to grab-and-go if necessary. Make sure that all family members know where the kit is stored, and can access it.

Tools and Supplies Kit

Rotation: As used
Storage: Portable container; located in a designated location known to all family members

❑ Portable radio/NOAA weather radio (if possible)	❑ Emergency Survival Book
❑ Extra batteries	❑ Shovel
❑ Flashlight	❑ Pliers/screwdrivers
❑ Matches (in waterproof bag)	❑ Nails/hammer
❑ Waterproof tarp (for tent or to cover damage)	❑ Disposable dust masks
❑ Fire extinguisher	❑ Axe
❑ Medium sized plastic bucket with tight lid	❑ Map(s) of the area
❑ Games/books/entertainment	❑ Compass
❑ Work gloves	❑ Toilet paper
❑ Duct Tape	❑ Plastic garbage bags/ties
	❑ Household chlorine bleach
❑ _____	❑ Disinfectant
❑ _____	❑ Plastic (for chemical release)
❑ _____	❑ _____
❑ _____	❑ _____
❑ _____	❑ _____
❑ _____	❑ _____
❑ _____	❑ _____
❑ _____	❑ _____
❑ _____	❑ _____
❑ _____	❑ _____
❑ _____	❑ _____

Customized Kits

Set up customized kits for anything specific to your family and its members – humans or pets – which is not covered by any of the common kits. Some examples of customized kits include jewelry (such as family heirlooms), special collections (e.g., statuettes or matchbox cars), special medical needs, religion-related needs, pet-carrying cases, etc.

Alternate benefit

If you prepare the full survival kit, items stored in the kit can be used as a backup when you run out of or cannot find an item for everyday use.

For example, if you lose or break your eyeglasses, you can use the extra pair of glasses in your Personal Pack until you are able to replace (or find) your good pair.

Don't forget though – you MUST remember to replace whatever you took from the kit as soon as possible.

In conclusion, here are a few general suggestions regarding your kits:

- Be sure everyone knows where they are stored, and can access them. The person who put the kits together may not be at home when disaster strikes, or may not survive. If no one else knows where the kits are stored, all the work that has been done in putting them together is wasted.

- Get the whole family involved with assembling these kits. In particular, allow each member to put together their Personal Pack (with assistance where small children or elderly people are concerned). This way, all family members know about the kits, and can have their questions answered well before they need to use these packs. This can be used to comfort children and calm their fears as to what might happen in a disaster.

- For those of you with pets, be sure to include them in your planning. As you saw after Hurricane Katrina, pets depend on humans for their survival.

The next collection task involves your home inventory. This will be critical to your recovery process following any event that impacts your household goods.

19

Home Inventory

Home is home, be it ever so humble.
PROVERB

Let me paint a picture of what could happen if you were to lose some or all of the contents of your home.

Even if you have the best insurance company and best insurance adjustor in the world, you will be asked for the following information prior to any checks being written to enable you to replace your losses:

- Name, address (permanent or temporary) and telephone numbers where they can reach you
- Inventory of lost and/or damaged items, including make, model, and serial number
- Description of the loss
- Pictures of the damage
- Reports from fire and/or police departments
- Reports from witnesses

Once you submit your paperwork, your insurance company then offers you a settlement. This will depend on the type of insurance you have purchased:

- **Cash Value** – only pays you the value of your loss in today's dollars. For example, you paid $1,000 for your stereo 10 years ago, but today it is only worth $300. You get the $300.

- **Replacement Value** – pays you sufficient to replace your assets in today's dollars. For example, the cost of replacing your stereo (for which you paid $1,000 ten years ago) at today's prices is $1,500. You get the $1,500.

- **Guaranteed Replacement Cost Insurance** – pays for rebuilding your home and replacing all your contents, no matter what the cost. Let's say your home and contents originally cost $275,000, but to replace everything today would cost $525,000. With this type of policy, you get the $525,000 (actually, you get everything replaced).

- **Extended Replacement Cost Insurance** – pays a certain amount above your policy limit. The extra amount is designed to cover rebuilding and replacement following a widespread disaster, when costs may be at a premium because of the high demand for and scarcity of labor and supplies.

If your insurance company offers a settlement and you accept immediately, you may only get one check, or you may receive up to four different checks. These include an advance check for immediate use, a temporary living expenses check, a check for any structural damage, and a check for personal property loss. If your house is mortgaged, the check you receive for structural damage may be made out to you *and* your lender.

Homeowners generally purchase their insurance annually to cover the house, garage and any other structures on the property. Insurance can be taken out to cover these assets in the event of any number of natural disasters you might experience, such as fire, flood, hurricane, etc. In addition, a homeowner's policy covers the contents of these structures. Most homeowners also include personal liability clauses protecting the homeowner from injury or damage to other people and their property. Additional riders – supplemental coverage that is purchased separately – can alter how all of these items are covered. Homeowners can also purchase loss-of-use coverage which pays for expenses incurred should they need to move out while their home is being repaired following a disaster.

Renters, on the other hand, may purchase renter's insurance, which does *not* cover structural damage, but can include coverage for personal liability, household goods, additional riders and loss of use.

Just having insurance cover, however, is not enough. While you can purchase whatever you feel you need to cover your home and its contents, the first thing your insurance company will require following any disaster is a full inventory of everything that has been lost. Do you really think you could compile an accurate inventory of the entire contents of your household from memory if they were suddenly destroyed? Don't forget, you may be sitting in a shelter after losing everything you own bar the clothes on your back. This is not the ideal situation in which to be compiling a full and accurate inventory of your life possessions, and it is inevitable that you will overlook some things, and thereby take a loss.

What to include

The following list outlines the areas you need to include when preparing your inventory of your home contents:

- Attic
- Basement
- Living Room
- Kitchen
- Master Bedroom/ Other Bedrooms
- Master Bath/ Other Bathrooms
- Dining Room
- All closets

- Garage
- Storage Units (on and off property)
- Outdoor/Landscaping/Pool
- Electronics
- Software/Computers
- Tools
- Collectibles (includes jewelry, furs, etc.)
- Safe Deposit Box

You need to list every item, the year it was purchased, the cost when purchased, the present value, its replacement value and a description (which includes make/model information and serial numbers). The best case scenario includes a sales slip and/or a picture of the item.

Inventory

A more specific list of suggestions about compiling an inventory of your home's contents follows. I have shown items as being in particular locations based on my own situation, but you might have the same items in different rooms. The important thing is that you customize these lists to ensure that *every* item you own makes it onto your inventory.

- **Attic**

| Furniture | Trunks |
| Boxes | Holiday/Home Decorations |

- **Basement**

Clothes Washer/Dryer	Laundry Equipment/Supplies
Hand Tools	Power Tools
Workbench	Supplies
Other Equipment	Furniture
Fuel	Heating Unit

Tables
Knick-Knacks
Rugs (free standing)

Trunks/Contents
Pictures/wall hangings
Window Treatments

- **Living Room**

Bookcases/Books
Chairs
Closet Contents
Desk
Lamps
Knick-Knacks
Piano/Instruments
Rugs (free standing)
Wall Shelves

Cabinets/contents
Clocks
Couches
Fireplace Equipment
Mirrors
Pictures/wall hangings
Pillows
Tables
Window Treatments

- **Kitchen**

Cabinet/drawer contents
Chairs
Closet contents
Dishwasher
Floor covering (free standing)
Freezer
Linens
Knick-Knacks
Refrigerator
Tables
Wall shelves
Water filter system

Cabinets – free standing
Clocks
Dishes/glasses
Electrical appliances
Food stuffs
Household utensils
Microwave
Pictures/wall hangings
Stove
Trash compactor
Window treatments
Garbage disposal

- **Master Bedroom/Bedrooms**

Bedding/Linens
Box spring
Chest of drawers
Closet built-ins
Desk
Knick-Knacks

Bookcases/Books
Chairs
Clocks
Contents of drawers and closets
Dressing table
Lamps

Mattress
Pictures/wall hangings
Tables
Window Treatments

Mirrors
Rugs (free standing)
Wall Shelves

- **Master Bath/Bathrooms**

Cabinets (free standing)
Electrical appliances
Scales
Chairs
Dressing table
Lamps
Pictures/wall hangings
Show Curtains

Contents (towels, etc.)
Linens
Toiletry articles
Closet contents
Knick-Knacks
Mirrors
Rugs (free standing)
Window treatments

- **Dining Room**

Buffet/contents
Chairs
China hutch
Closet/contents
Knick-knacks
Pictures/wall hangings
Rugs (free standing)
Silverware
Table linens

Cabinets/contents
China
Clocks
Crystal
Lamps
Mirrors
Server
Table
Window treatments

- **Home Office/Den**

Bookcases/books
Clock
Filing cabinets
Lamps
Paintings/pictures/wall hangings
Tables
Window treatments

Chairs
Desk
Knick-Knacks
Office supplies
Rugs (free standing)
Wall shelves

- **Garage**

  Auto equipment/tools
  Other tools
  Lawnmower
  Leaf removal
  Cabinets/contents
  Recreational vehicle(s)

  Garden tools
  Storage/boxes/contents
  Snow removal
  Power washer
  Car trunk contents

- **Storage Units**

  Cabinets/contents
  Furniture

  Boxes/contents
  Other items

- **Outdoor/Landscaping**

  Outdoor furniture
  Refrigeration units
  Chemicals
  Security/fencing/lighting
  Storage boxes

  Cooking units/utensils
  Pools/toys/tools
  Yard games/play area
  Shrubs/plantings

- **Electronics**

  Camera(s)
  Outdoor entertainment
  PC (desktop and laptop)
  Radio / stereo / sound system / speaker
  Hand-held devices
  Answering machine(s)
  Wireless devices
  Calculators

  Video equipment
  Cell phones
  Printer/scanner/fax/copier
  Televisions
  Video games/devices
  I-pod(s)
  Recording Devices

- **Software**

  Programs (with versions)
  Operating systems (with versions)

  Games
  Specialty software

- **Tools**

Basic	Measuring/leveling
Table saws	Painting supplies
Ladders	Hobby Tools

- **Collectibles**

Figurines	Stamps
Books	CDs/DVDs
Craftworks	

Inventory of part-time members

Part-time members who live away from home (at school or college) should also do an inventory (they really need their *own* emergency plan) for their usual place of residence. Likewise, members who travel a lot should have an inventory of items they carry with them, such as their own personal laptop, cell phone, jewelry, etc. Keep in mind, if something happens to one of your family members, full-time or part-time, you need to be able to identify what they had with them, and therefore what might have been lost or stolen.

Following is an example of an inventory sheet you can use to assist the process. Remember, the quicker you get this done, the sooner your family is better protected. Before you begin this task, be sure to review the *Time-wise options* options that follow.

To use this form, make as many copies as you need, enter the room/location at the top of each sheet, and simply list the entire contents of that room/location.

Inventory for _____
(location / room)

# of items	Item	Year Purchased	Original Cost	Present Value	Replacement Value	Description

Time-wise options

There are several high-tech options available to help you prepare your inventory. As you read through them, you may want to mix-and-match depending on what electronic equipment you have available. It's your choice.

I would also suggest you check with your insurance carrier to see what formats they accept. Keep in mind, you may be required to translate – in essence, handwrite – your list from your electronic format before your insurance company will accept a claim or cut a check. Any of these methods will definitely save you a lot of time up front, and ensure that you are fully prepared.

- **Video Tape** – use a video camera to record the contents of your home. Don't forget to open up closets and drawers. Focus on titles of books/CDs/DVDs/VHS tapes so you could read their names should you need to make a list. Focus on serial numbers for electronics when available. Verbalize information such as year purchased, original cost, present value and replacement value while you are recording.

  o When you have completed the entire inventory (including your garage, attic, basement, yard, etc.) store the tape offsite (a safe deposit box is a good idea). Ideally, you should also make a backup copy of the tape. Ensure that the backup is stored in a cool, dry place that you can access easily if required.

  o Bear in mind, this option requires you to have a way to play-back the video for your insurance company.

- **Digital Photos** – use a digital camera to record the contents of your home. Don't forget to open up closets and drawers. Focus on the titles of books/CDs/DVDs/VHS tapes. Focus on serial numbers for electronics if these are available. If there is time, caption the photos with make/model number, purchase date, original cost, etc. If possible, download to a CD/DVD for storage. Make multiple copies and take them to several different offsite locations (safe deposit box, your office desk, a relative's house, etc.). Store copies in a cool, dry place where they can be easily accessed if required. Another option is to send the photos to yourself in an e-mail. Be sure to store them properly so they remain in your e-mail file and are available if required. Bear in mind, this option requires you to have a way for your insurance company to view the photos.

- **Film Photos** – Record the contents of you home using a film camera. Don't forget to open up closets and drawers. Focus on titles of books/CDs/DVDs/VHS tapes. Focus on serial numbers of electronics when available. Have duplicate copies printed, and when you get the photos back, write the details for each item, such as the year it was purchased, original cost, present value and replacement value on the back of each photo. Take the negatives and one set of prints to separate offsite locations. Store them in a cool, dry place where they can be easily accessed if required.

  o **NOTE:** You can purchase several rolls of film, photograph the whole house, and submit them all at once for processing, or if you take pictures on a regular basis, use the last few frames on each roll of film to take pictures of your contents. Be aware however that you need to capture the entire contents as a starting point, so this approach will really only be useful for updates when you purchase new items.

- **Soft Copy List** – If you have access to any spreadsheet or word processing software, you can record your inventory using this software. A copy of the entire list can then be backed up and stored offsite. Copies can easily be sent to relatives (or to your own e-mail storage) for backup. This list would then be able to be printed out and submitted to your insurance carrier. This method can be used in conjunction with any of the aforementioned options. It is highly recommended that you thoroughly document your most expensive items by either retaining receipts or keeping a visual record (photos or videos). Bottom line, before your insurance carrier reimburses you for the loss of that fabulous 60" plasma screen television, they need you to prove you actually owned it in the first place – not an unreasonable position.

- **Handwritten List** – You may elect to handwrite your entire inventory. You can then either take photocopies or scan the handwritten pages into your computer to create backup copies. Again, you may want to confirm ownership of your larger items either by retaining the receipt or through photos or videos.

- **Online Options** – if you have access to the internet, you will find several online sites that provide information about collecting your inventory. Use these sites to record and store your information for future reference.

Budget-wise options

The cheapest way to complete your inventory is to handwrite it using copies of the form provided a few pages back, and the least expensive way to prove ownership of the items on your list is to either save your receipts, or ensure you have at least one picture of each room in your home. I read one story of a family who lost everything in Hurricane Katrina but they were able to compile a list for their insurance company by using photos that had been taken during a family gathering just a few weeks earlier. These photos helped when submitting their claim forms. If you already have current photos of each room in your home, use these as proof of ownership to accompany your inventory lists.

These Budget-wise options options take more time up front to put together but are the quickest way to provide the required information when submitting a claim.

You may want to use a combination of methods for your inventory. For example, you might video tape your inventory immediately, to ensure that you have an up-to-date record of your home and all its contents. Then, as you purchase new items, you might enter the details on a handwritten list, and keep the receipts. You may want to record a new video or set of photographs every year from this point forward, to ensure your supporting evidence for your inventory lists is up-to-date. Think about what works best for you and your family, and about how quickly you want to be able to lodge a claim should something happen.

If you decide to handwrite your inventory, you might want to consider the following:

- Do one room per week. Don't try to do the whole house at once. Instead, approach the exercise in smaller chunks.

- Another option is to do it by item category. For example, start with your expensive electronic equipment. Once you have listed these, make sure you have photos and/or receipts to prove you own them. The next category might be your furniture. Ditto on the pictures and/or receipts. This can be followed by entertainment items like books, CDs and DVDs. Continue until everything is catalogued. Again, be sure to have proof of ownership, especially in relation to the high-value items.

- Everyone has a closet or some other place where *stuff* collects. As part of updating your inventory, clean out this area annually and donate unwanted items, THEN do your inventory. This approach reduces the number of items you need to keep track of and, if you donate the goods, gives you a possible financial benefit in the form of a tax write-off. Talk with your accountant about this one.

- Solicit help from each family member to document the inventory in their own bedrooms.

Alternate benefit

An accurate and up-to-date inventory of exactly what you have in your home is a valuable tool that helps you determine how much insurance you need to purchase. Use your inventory list to determine, with the help of your agent, whether you need any type of specialty insurance. You can purchase exactly what you need, rather than trying to *guess* at what you need, possibly either wasting money or worse, leaving yourself under-insured and therefore vulnerable.

Also, having compiled your inventory list, you will understand why purchasing replacement insurance makes a lot of sense.

When you decide to donate items to your favorite charity, your list provides you with a way to quickly identify the item's value. When the time comes to list the total of your charitable contributions on your tax return, the backup information is readily available. This may also come in very handy if you are ever audited.

Another benefit of doing an annual inventory is that it encourages you to clean out your closets every year. You can tie your closet clean out to *holiday giving* by timing it for November/December. Each family member should clean out their own closet, identifying and discarding items that they no longer use. The inventory list is then updated by deleting these items. A list of items to be donated is then compiled, complete with values, and the items are donated prior to December 31. It's a win-win-win. You win because your closets are cleaned out. You also win with a timely tax write-off. And, the charity wins because they have new items with which to help the needy.

Bear in mind, whenever you amend your inventory, you may also need to adjust your Will, preferably at least annually, to ensure it is up to date.

Compiling an inventory is not hard, and it provides numerous valuable benefits. I urge you to do one today.

20

Critical Records

The palest ink is better than the best memory.
CHINESE PROVERB

No matter who you are, and whether you're rich or poor, young or old, male or female, married or single, you have at least *some* critical records. For recovery purposes following any disaster, it is important that you identify these records, know where the originals are stored, and have ready access to at least a copy.

What is a critical record?

For the purposes of this book, a critical record is one that confirms your identity, establishes ownership (for example a title deed), confirms a legal entitlement, or marks a milestone in your life.

A good example of a critical record is your driver's license. This is generally used for identification, but can also represent evidence of a major milestone in your life – the legal right to drive a car!

Financial records will be discussed in the next chapter.

Examples

There are many examples of critical records, depending on your life experiences. The following is a list of the most common ones:

- **Birth Certificate** – government-issued document identifying date and place of birth, and identity of parents. This document is often required as proof of identity before you can obtain many other documents, such as a passport or various types of licenses.

- **Driver's License** – state-issued document identifying name, address, general description, donor status, and types of vehicles authorized to drive.

- **Vehicle Registration** – state-issued document identifying your vehicle. Includes license plate number.

- **Passport** – federally-issued document that includes a photo, and is used by other governments to identify you and permit legal entry into their country.

- **Naturalization Papers** – federally-issued document which confirms that you have been granted citizenship.

- **Will or Living Trust** – documents assigning legal transfer of property and other assets and care of surviving dependants in the event of your death. NOTE: consider making sure three other documents are completed with your Will: Living Will, Durable Power of Attorney and Durable Power of Attorney for Healthcare, each of which is described below.

- **Living Will** – may also be called a Healthcare Directive or Directive to Physician. This document spells out the type and extent of treatment you want if you enter a coma or vegetative state, whether through an accident or a terminal condition.

- **Durable Power of Attorney** – this document is used to authorize a person to make financial and legal decisions on your behalf should you become incapacitated.

- **Durable Power of Attorney for Healthcare** – sometimes called a Healthcare Proxy. This document is used to authorize a person to make medical decisions on your behalf should you become incapacitated.

- **Social Security Card** – federally-issued document showing your assigned social security number. This is your primary means of identification for government-related purposes.

- **Marriage Certificate** – state-issued document identifying date and place of marriage, together with names of the couple, witnesses, and officiator.

- **Pre-Nuptial Agreement** – document prepared and signed by both parties prior to marriage assigning division of assets should the marriage be dissolved.

- **Partnership Agreement/License** – state-issued document identifying date and place partnership was entered into, together with names of partners, witnesses and officiator.

- **Divorce Decree** – state-issued document identifying names of the divorcing couple, date and place, and reason for divorce.

- **Custody Papers** – state-issued document assigning parenting rights.

- **Adoption Papers** – government-issued document assigning parenting rights.

- **Degrees/Diplomas** – school/university-issued documents identifying name, date and degree conferred.

- **Military Papers/Release** – federally-issued documents confirming name, rank, dates and nature of service, and date and status of discharge.

- **Employment Agreement** – company-issued document identifying name, and dates and parameters of employment and/or termination.

- **Resume** – paper or electronic copy of the most up-to-date employment history.

- **Vehicle Title** – state-issued document confirming ownership of vehicle.

- **Home Deed** – state-issued document confirming ownership of property.

- **Death Certificate** – state-issued document listing name, date, place and cause of death.

- **Certificate of Authenticity** – document confirming the authenticity of an item. Examples include paintings, sports memorabilia, stamps, etc.

Depending on your circumstances, you may identify additional documents that you consider critical. When you add this information to your family plan, be sure to include these additional documents.

What do I need to do with them?

First, you need to answer the following questions:

- Which family members have which documents?

- Is there a number or unique identifier for each document (for example each driver's license has a unique number)?

- Where is the original kept?

- Where is the backup copy kept (you should have copies of each of these documents)?

- How can I or someone else obtain a replacement, or at least obtain information that might be required (especially if you are gone)

Then what?

Once you have identified who has which documents, where the originals are stored, and where to find a copy, you can incorporate this information into your family plan.

For example, if both your passport and your driver's license are destroyed in a disaster, it will be a lot easier to replace these documents if you can access copies. You may also be able to use the copy as a temporary form of identification immediately following the event, but you would need to check with your local authorities and your insurance carrier to be sure.

Control of critical documents is probably most important when someone dies. Consider the following examples:

- **Custody Papers** – Let's assume you and your spouse were divorced, and there was a custody dispute, after which you were awarded full custody of your children. If you were to die in a car accident, your family would need access to these papers if they were going to continue taking care of your children (assuming this is your wish).

- **Pre-Nuptial Agreement** – if you are like me, and not rich, you may think you don't need a pre-nuptial agreement. However what if you re-married, and each of you had children from previous marriages. After moving in with you, your new spouse might sell their home and give the proceeds to their children, and then, when you die, unless you have specified otherwise, *your* children will *not* get your house – your spouse will. This is why you need a pre-nuptial agreement. Property that is jointly owned (in this case with your spouse) cannot be left to someone else in your Will. So, even if you are not rich, you may still need a pre-nuptial agreement, and you need to let your family know where the copies are kept!

- **Living Will** – Each of us should set out our wishes for medical treatment should we become incapacitated – *before* we have an accident or are struck down by a stroke. You need to be very specific if you want them to do everything possible to keep you alive, even if it means using artificial means. And, if you want a particular person to make medical decisions on your behalf should you become incapacitated, you need to say so, otherwise the courts may get to make the final decision.

Alternate benefit

Keeping important documents stored in designated areas makes them easy to find. For example, if you always store your passport in a specific location, it's easy to locate whenever you need to travel out of the country.

The important documents confirming ownership (home deeds and car titles) will be needed if you decide to sell these assets. If you know where they are located, the sale process is much easier, and it may even mean the difference between taking advantage of a great offer and missing out.

Time-wise options

Here are some time-saver options for recording your critical records:

- **Soft Copy of Details** – If you have access to spreadsheet or word processing software, you can use this to record information about your critical records. A copy can then be made and stored offsite, and can also be e-mailed to relatives as a backup.

- **Soft Copy of Documents** – Scan each document into your computer, then print out and/or burn a copy onto CD/DVD. Store the copy offsite. If you want, you can e-mail another copy to a relative as a backup.

- **Send a copy to an e-mail storage address.** There are several options for setting up free e-mail addresses offering storage space, enabling you to simply send an e-mail to yourself with each document attached. Your copies are then easily accessible, assuming you or someone else can access your e-mail address (don't forget to let someone know about it!).

Budget-wise options

If you don't have facilities to copy or scan the documents, you can record information about your critical documents manually. Use the *Critical Records* form to record details of all critical documents for each family member. If you decide you don't want to, or are unable to, make any backup copies, note where the original is located. Examples include the relevant state or federal government office, your attorney's or accountant's office, etc. So, even though you don't have a copy readily available, you have instructions on where and how to access the original if it is needed.

Critical Records for _____
(member name)

	Document Name:	Document Name:	Document Name:
Name on Document			
Identification #			
Location of Original			
Location of Copy			
Retrieval Notes:			
	Document Name:	Document Name:	Document Name:
Name on Document			
Identification #			
Location of Original			
Location of Copy			
Retrieval Notes:			
	Document Name:	Document Name:	Document Name:
Name on Document			
Identification #			
Location of Original			
Location of Copy			
Retrieval Notes:			

You may need to retrieve some of these documents immediately following a disaster, while others may be able to wait until time permits.

Where any of your critical documents appear as a resource on your emergency plan, identify who is assigned to obtain the document, either the original or the copy. This person needs to know where the original and any copies are located, and should be familiar with the procedure required to obtain the original, a backup copy, or a replacement. They must also be authorized to access the document(s) if they are stored in something like a safe-deposit box. In cases where access is required to secure areas, you might feel safer having two backup people who are allowed to access the document(s).

Be careful where you store your Critical Records information list. Many items on the list, such as those including your Social Security or account numbers, would leave you extremely vulnerable if they were to fall into the wrong hands.

Next, we move on to collecting additional personal information for each family member.

21

Personal Records

A little fact is worth a whole limbo of dreams.
RALPH WALDO EMERSON

Personal records are different from the critical records discussed in the previous chapter, in that these are everyday records. The primary purpose of this chapter is to make sure this additional information is collected and stored in one or more places, so that your family (or someone else, if your entire family is hit by a disaster) can easily put their hands on this information if required.

What is a personal record?

Everyone has personal records. These are the documents you use in the course of living your everyday life. While most people are likely to have their critical documents in order, many people overlook these other records.

Let me give you an example. I pay my bills using my credit union's automatic bill pay system. This is a very convenient system, and means I don't have to think about these bills, but if I were to be incapacitated or die, I would want someone to go in there and STOP the payments. This is an easy enough request – so long as someone knows my credit union's web site address, my log-in details, and the procedure required to cancel automatic bill pay.

It's these types of everyday records that we are now talking about. They are very important if your family is going to be able to recover from a disaster in an orderly fashion.

Examples

Examples of personal records include:

- **General Information** – information about each family member, such as their social security number, date and place of birth, names of parents, siblings, etc.

- **Insurance** – specific details on all types of insurance purchased by or for this family member (life, car, home, other).

- **Medical Records** – identify doctors, supply a medical overview (blood type, any conditions or allergies), list medication for each member.

- **Retirement Records** – identify locations and account numbers of 401(k), pension, investments, IRA(s), savings plans, etc.

- **Log-in Records** – all user name and password combinations for critical websites such as bank accounts, credit cards/financial records, etc.

- **School Records** – report cards, certificates, awards and other documents which may be needed to verify qualifications and achievements.

- **Subscriptions/Loyalty Program Records** – details of all subscriptions (newspapers, magazines, etc.) to enable cancellation or redirection as required, and loyalty programs, so benefits can be transferred (if permitted).

- **E-mail/Friends/Contacts Address Lists** – have you ever lost your entire e-mail address book? Make backup lists of important addresses and contact information, both electronic and physical, for friends and other contacts. Most e-mail programs allow you to print a copy of your address list.

- **Scheduled Activities** – Do you have any activities or events which occur on a regular schedule? Examples include lawn services, sporting activities, church activities, social groups, medical services such as massages or pedicures, scheduled home maintenance, car maintenance, etc. Also, have you made any one-off arrangements that are to be completed at a later date, such as a trip (on which a deposit may have been paid), an appointment with a specialist, etc.? Having access to this information enables someone to step in and take appropriate action on your behalf should disaster strike.

- **Vehicle/Maintenance Records** – collect information on every vehicle owned by members of your family, including cars, trucks, motorcycles, planes, recreational vehicles and boats. Be sure to include scheduled maintenance records. If you happen to have play vehicles, include the details.

- **Property Records** – list details of all property owned by each family member.

- **Financial Records** – list information relating to your bank accounts, creditors, debtors, etc.

- **Funeral Arrangements** – write down what needs to be done to farewell each family member, including music, burial arrangements (pre-paid or not), who needs to be contacted, etc.

You should add any other personal records that are specific to your family members and have not been covered in this list.

Different types of information are required for each of these categories, as outlined in the following section.

What information should I collect?

As you read through this section, you need to keep in mind the need to collect each type of information for every family member (where appropriate). Although this may seem like a daunting task, I recommend that each family member collect his or her own information if possible, which makes it much easier.

- *General Information* – Gather the following general information:
    - o Social Security Number
    - o Date of Birth
    - o City of Birth
    - o Mother's Name (including Maiden Name)
    - o Father's Name
    - o Siblings
    - o Armed Force Branch/#
    - o Degrees
    - o Colleges
    - o Occupation/Title

You need this information if you are required to collect benefits on behalf of a family member, or if you have to write an obituary. Having these details written down means you can move forward as and when required.

Member General Information for _____
(member name)

Member Name	
Social Security Number	
Birth Date	
Parents' Names	
Spouse's Name	
Siblings	
Children	
Other Notable Relatives	
Schools/Degrees	
Armed Forces Detail	

- *Insurance* – When thinking about insurance, be sure to add any other types of insurance you might have purchased that are not listed here:
  - o **Home/Rental Property, Life, Car, Pet Insurance** – Insurance company, address, phone, contact name, policy number, location of policy papers, description of coverage
  - o **Medical Health Savings Account** – Company, address, phone, contact name, account number, location of account papers, description of account, etc. Although this is a savings account, it is used to pay medical expenses not covered by insurance, so consider it as an insurance supplement.
  - o **Long-Term Health Care Coverage** – Company, address, phone, contact name, account number, location of account papers, description of account, etc. This type of coverage often has a payback clause if the insured dies without having used part or all of the coverage.

Insurance Information for: _____
(member name)

Type of Insurance					
Insurance Company					
Policy Number					
Contact Name					
Contact Telephone Number					
Contact E-mail					
Address					
City/State/Zip					
Location of Policy					
Description of Coverage					

- *Medical Records* – Some of this information is included in your Wallet Communications Plan, but this is in case that form is destroyed for any reason (think Hurricane Katrina):

    o **Doctors** (contact information for general, optical, dental, specialists, etc.)

    o **Pharmacist(s)** (contact information)

    o **General medical overview** (list blood type, hospitalizations, serious illnesses, conditions, allergies, etc. including current general health status)

    o **Medications** (list all current medications, including dosages)

    o **X-rays** (contact information)

Medical Records for: _____
(member name)

Page 1 of 2

Doctor's Name					
Practice Name					
Medical Record Number					
Address					
City/State/Zip					
Telephone Number (office)					
Telephone Number (alternate)					
E-mail Address					
Notes:					

Medical Records for: _____

(member name)

Page 2 of 2

Medical Overview: List all allergies, drug use, birth defects, eating disorders, pregnancies, obesity, smoker, etc.	
Medication/Notes/Comments:	
Hospitalization/Notes/Comments:	
Serious Illness/Notes/Comments	
Dental or Eye Notes/Comments	
Location of X-rays/Notes/Comments	
Other Notes:	

- *Retirement Records* – Many people invest in several plans for their retirement. Details should be collected on:

    o **401(k)** – contact information, account information, sponsor, etc. for each 401(k) plan

    o **IRA** – contact information, account information, sponsor, etc. for each IRA (Roth or Regular) plan

    o **ESOP** - contact information, account information, sponsor, etc. for each employee stock option plan

    o **Pension** – contact information, account information, sponsor, etc. for each pension plan

    o **Investments** – contact information, specific details, etc. for any retirement investments

    o **Employment Contract** – if your employment contract includes retirement benefits, be sure to identify this as part of your personal records and/or critical records

Retirement Records for: _____
(member name)

Account Name:				
Name(s) on Account				
Account #				
Address				
City/State/Zip				
Telephone				
E-mail				
Website				
User name/Password				
Payout Notes including beneficiary name(s):				

- *Log-in List* – have you ever forgotten a password? This list may prove to be a life-saver, either for you, or for your family, should you die or be incapacitated. Things to include are:
    - o **Website Name/Purpose**
    - o **URL** (website address)
    - o **User Name/Password**
    - o **Account Information** (if applicable)
    - o **ATM Cards** (PIN numbers)

        Remember, this information could do a lot of damage in the wrong hands, so make sure it is kept in a secure location and can only be accessed by nominated people.

Log-In/Online Records for: _____
(member name)

Website Name	Purpose	Site Address/URL	User ID/Log-in	Password	Account Number	Monthly Fee/How Paid	Other Notes

- *Subscriptions/Loyalty Programs* – Everyone can identify with something on this list. We all have miles traveled, or magazine subscriptions, or 'points' on credit or store cards. Do you know what you have? If something should happen to you, wouldn't you want any accumulated benefits transferred to your family for:

  o **Airline Loyalty Programs** – contact information, account details, transfer/cancellation information, etc.

  o **Hotel Loyalty Programs** – contact information, account details, upon-death disbursement, etc.

  o **Car Rental Programs** – contact information, account details, transfer/cancellation information, etc.

  o **Store Loyalty Programs** – contact information, account details, transfer/cancellation information, etc.

  o **Credit Card Loyalty Programs** – contact information, account details, transfer/cancellation information, etc.

  o **Other Loyalty Programs** – contact information, account details, upon-death disbursement, etc.

  o **Subscriptions** – contact information, subscription details, transfer/cancellation information, etc.

  o **Season Tickets** – contact information, event details, transfer/cancellation information, etc.

Subscription/Loyalty Records for: _____

(member name)

Program			
Name on Account			
Account Number			
Disposition at my death			
Annual Cost			
Website Address			
Telephone Number(s)			
Address/City/State/Zip			
Notes			

- *Scheduled Activities* – We all have appointments, payments, and activities scheduled in advance. Should something happen, they will need to be cancelled, and people notified. Again, this is a very easy task, so long as someone knows about it, and has the necessary information:

  o **Travel bookings** – contact information, amount pre-paid, amount due, due date, travel details, cancellation insurance (if purchased), transfer/cancellation information, etc.

  o **Monthly Payments** – contact information, due date, amount due, description, etc. This may include such things as home-owners' associations, internet connectivity, club memberships, DVD rentals, gyms, websites, etc.

  o **Regularly-Scheduled Activities** – contact information, amounts pre-paid or due if applicable, activity details, etc. This may include such things as massage, yoga, church activities, school activities, etc.

  o **Regularly-Scheduled Services** – contact information, amounts pre-paid or due if applicable, service details, etc. Consider such things as yard, pool or gutter cleaning, car maintenance, heating oil delivery, air conditioner/heater service, etc.

  o **Pet Services** – contact information, amount pre-paid/due if applicable, dates, details of service, etc.

Scheduled Activities: _____
(member name)

Member Name	Activity	Scheduled Time(s) / Due Date(s)	Contact Information	Cost	Form of Payment	Other Notes

- *Vehicle Records* – Sometimes, a family allocates the household duties, and one person is placed in charge of the vehicle maintenance. Should something happen to that person, or the records are lost (by either the family or the dealership) or destroyed, the following information (car titles are part of the Critical Records) would be good to have on hand:
  - o **Description/Color** – model, make, year and color of the vehicle
  - o **VIN** – the Vehicle Identification Number
  - o **Retail Value** – current retail value of the vehicle
  - o **Location** – the usual physical location of the vehicle and appropriate contact information
  - o **Names on Title** – list the names shown on the official vehicle title
  - o **License Number** – the number shown on the license plate of this vehicle
  - o **Notes** – any other details about the car and its history.

Vehicle Records for: _____
(member name)

	Vehicle 1	Vehicle 2	Vehicle 3	Vehicle 4
Make/Model				
VIN				
Location				
Owner(s)				
Insurer (see details with insurance information)				
Finance company and location				
Loan #				
Payment Details				
Location of vehicle title				
Maintenance Details				

- *Property Records* – Although property titles should be included with Critical Records, the following day-to-day information should be recorded about each property:
    o **Location** – the full address, city, state and zip, of each property
    o **Owners** – list the names on the Deed
    o **Mortgage Information** – mortgage company, contact information, loan number, etc.

Property Records for: _____
(member name)

Property Records	Property 1	Property 2	Property 3	Property 4
Address of property (street)				
City/State/Zip				
Owner(s)				
Mortgage Company				
Mortgage Company Address/City/State/Zip				
Loan #				
Mortgage Company Contact Information				
Payment Details				
Other Notes				

- *Financial Records* – List the following information for each family member:

  o **Money Owed** – list names, addresses, contact information, account numbers, due dates, amounts due, etc. for credit cards, taxes, car loans, mortgages, loans from family or friends, interest/notes, etc.

  o **Money Owing** – list names, addresses, contact information, account numbers, due dates, amounts due, etc. for tax refunds, loans to family or friends, vendor refunds, tickets to be refunded (airline, sports, theater, etc.) any payoff at death clauses (if the payable has *paid in full* at death coverage), interest/notes, etc.

Financial Records for: _____

Financial Records	Payable #1	Payable #2	Payable #3	Payable #4
Due To (name)				
Loan or account number				
Finance address/city/ state/zip				
Contact Name				
Telephone Number (s)				
E-mail and/or URL				
Payment Details				
Other Notes				

Financial Records for: _____

(member name)

Page 2 of 3

Financial Records	Receivable #1	Receivable #2	Receivable #3	Receivable #4
Due From (name)				
Loan #				
Address/City/State/ Zip				
Contact Name				
Telephone Number(s)				
E-mail or URL				
Payment Details				
Other Notes				

Financial Records for: _____

(member name)

Bank or Credit Union Check/Save Accounts	Account #1	Account #2	Account #3	Account #4
Name(s) on Account				
Account #				
Address/City/State/Zip				
Telephone Number(s)				
E-mail				
Website				
User name/Password				
Account Notes				

- *Pet Records* – Details of day-to-day care for pets is important to ensure they receive adequate care if required. Record the following:
  - o **Pet Name**
  - o **Species/Description/Breed/Sex**
  - o **Date of Birth**
  - o **Habitat** (identify if this is an indoor or outdoor pet)
  - o **Medical Preventatives/Vaccinations** – include information on heartworm preventative, flea preventative and vaccinations received, dates of last treatment and next scheduled date
  - o **Medical Treatments/Medications** – list any special medical treatments and medications, normal checkups, special medications including dosage and frequency, etc.
  - o **Other Notes** – include any other information you feel would help someone else take care of your pet if required.

Pet Medical Records – Cat

Pet Name			
Species			
Description/Breed			
Date of Birth			
Sex	FE FES M MC	FE FES M MC	FE FES M MC
Habitat	Indoor Outdoor	Indoor Outdoor	Indoor Outdoor
Heartworm Preventative	Yes No	Yes No	Yes No
Flea Preventative	Yes No	Yes No	Yes No
Vaccinations	FVRCP __/__/__ Heartworm Test __/__/__ FIV Test __/__/__ Fecal Exam __/__/__ Feline Leukemia __/__/__ Other: __/__/__	FVRCP __/__/__ Heartworm Test __/__/__ FIV Test __/__/__ Fecal Exam __/__/__ Feline Leukemia __/__/__ Other: __/__/__	FVRCP __/__/__ Heartworm Test __/__/__ FIV Test __/__/__ Fecal Exam __/__/__ Feline Leukemia __/__/__ Other: __/__/__
Medications/Notes			

Pet Medical Records – Dog

Pet Name			
Species			
Description/Breed			
Date of Birth			
Sex	FE FEES M MC	FE FEES M MC	FE FEES M MC
Habitat	Indoor Outdoor	Indoor Outdoor	Indoor Outdoor
Heartworm Preventative	Yes No	Yes No	Yes No
Flea Preventative	Yes No	Yes No	Yes No
Vaccinations	Distempar/Parvo __/__/__ Heartworm Test __/__/__ Rabies __/__/__ Bordetella (kennel cough) __/__/__ Fecal Exam __/__/__ Coronavirus __/__/__	Distempar/Parvo __/__/__ Heartworm Test __/__/__ Rabies __/__/__ Bordetella (kennel cough) __/__/__ Fecal Exam __/__/__ Coronavirus __/__/__	Distempar/Parvo __/__/__ Heartworm Test __/__/__ Rabies __/__/__ Bordetella (kennel cough) __/__/__ Fecal Exam __/__/__ Coronavirus __/__/__
Medications/Notes			

- *Funeral Arrangements* – as mentioned in Chapter 9 – *Loss of Adult Member*, talking about death is difficult for most people, but if you have written everything down, think how much easier it will be for your family. Include the following information:

    o **Funeral Home** – contact information, pre-paid amount, remaining amount due, document location, policy number, etc.

    o **Burial/Cemetery** – contact information, pre-paid amount, remaining amount due, document location, policy number, pall-bearers, music, readings, participants, etc.

    o **Saying Goodbye** – information about personal letters to family and friends telling them what they mean to you, in the event that death occurs unexpectedly and you have not verbalized your thoughts.

    o **Contact List** – names of people to contact in the event of death

Funeral Arrangements for: _____

(member name)

Page 1 of 2

Arrangements	Preparation	Service	Burial
Name			
Contact Name			
Telephone			
Address/City/State/Zip			
E-mail			
Detail Prepaid Arrangements			
Detail Amount Due			
Music:			
Readings:			

Funeral Arrangements for: _____

(member name)

Requested participants (pall bearers, readers, singers, etc.)	Obituary notes	Goodbye Letters Location/ Information	Upon Death, Contact:	Relationship	Telephone(s)	E-mail
			1.	1.	1.	1.
			2.	2.	2.	2.
			3.	3.	3.	3.
			4.	4.	4.	4.
			5.	5.	5.	5.
			6.	6.	6.	6.
			7.	7.	7.	7.
			8.	8.	8.	8.
			9.	9.	9.	9.
			10.	10.	10.	10.
			11.	11.	11.	11.
			12.	12.	12.	12.

Then what?

You need to collect the appropriate information for all your family members. Again, I strongly suggest you distribute copies of the forms and have each person do their own (so long as they understand what is required).

One note on making funeral preparations for your children – as uncomfortable as it may make you feel, do it now. Regularly ask them what their favorite song is (so it can be played at the service) and who their friends are (so you can contact them). Think about it. If you lost a child in a disaster or an accident, wouldn't it be a little easier if at least some of the preparations had been done? It would enable you to hand this information off to a friend to take care of things. One thing is for sure, if it wasn't written down, *you* would have to do all the work, not a pleasant prospect at what would surely be an extremely emotional time.

Time-wise options

The quickest way to collect this information and store it in one area is to download it or copy it, if possible. If you have a software program, or there is an online system like the US Health and Human Services Family Health Portrait (**https://familyhistory.hhs.gov/**) to store parts or all of this information, be sure you understand how long the records are maintained, how secure they are, and that there is a process that enables you to maintain them on a regular basis.

If you use an automated system for your personal accounting, quickly gather the information requested that may already be available on that system. You may find that some of the at-home accounting systems offer the functionality to allow you to collect and print easily.

Another option is to either key in or scan the information and then burn it onto a CD or DVD or send it to yourself in an e-mail as an attachment by way of backup. Ensure that at least one copy is kept offsite in case a disaster destroys your home.

Make sure someone else knows if its existence, and knows how and where to access it should it be needed.

Budget-wise options

The cheapest way to compile this information is to handwrite it. Make sure the forms are kept somewhere safe and, keep at least one copy offsite. The following pages contain examples of forms you can use to collect whatever personal information applies to your family members. If you have added extra steps to any of your plans of action, you should collect the relevant information at this time.

Think of how far you have come! Your family is so much better off now than when you first started writing your plan. You have two things left to do: test your plan to make sure everything works properly and set up a schedule to maintain it. It's time to see how well you did.

PHASE 4

Testing and Maintenance

Elizabeth M. Owen

Do you have to practice mock fire drills at work (or school) once or twice a year? How many of you groan when the alarm goes off, and you have to stop what you're doing and hike down the stairs to meet at a designated point outside the building? Doesn't it always seem to happen when you are so busy you don't even have time to go to the bathroom, or the weather is inclement – it's either raining, snowing, or extremely hot or humid? 'What's that all about?' you may be thinking. Sometimes you may wonder if it's a conspiracy.

However, have you ever had to evacuate a building in response to a real emergency? I have, and let me tell you, when you don't know why the alarm is going off, you feel so glad you know what to do and where to go. This is made possible by the regular fire drills.

You have now come to the point in preparing your emergency plan where the rubber meets the road. You need to test your plan to make sure it works as you intended. There is no better time than when you are calm, and not under pressure, to test your plan. If you find there are flaws or oversights in your plan, no harm, no foul. You simply adjust your plan accordingly. But the only way you will know whether or not it is going to stand up in a real-life situation is to actually test it. Most importantly, testing gives each family member a chance to practice all the steps they are required to take without undue pressure. All family members learn how to get to safety quickly, which increases their chances of survival and recovery.

The good news is, you do *not* have to test every single plan of action. You only need to test those plans that involve a life and death situation.

Once you know your plan works, the only remaining task is to make sure that it is kept up to date. Our lives are constantly changing. People marry, others get divorced. Babies are born, and you send your 'babies' off to school or college. New homes are purchased, and renovations are made. And people die. No matter who you are, your life is constantly changing.

Any emergency plan that is not kept up to date quickly becomes worthless. Let me give you an example. If you list the emergency numbers to call in the event that one of your credit cards is stolen, but don't check them regularly, there is always a possibility that the numbers will change. That is not something you want to discover when disaster strikes. Regular checks ensure that you can easily make any required adjustments, and your plan will continue to give you and your family protection.

To help you in regularly testing your plan, and keeping it maintained, I have prepared a 12-month activity calendar. The tasks you need to do regularly to test your plan and keep it up-to-date have been spread throughout the year, with only two blocks of activities assigned to specific months, those for April and October (tied to when we change the clock). The remaining activities can be assigned across the other ten months in whatever way is most suitable for you and your family. In any case, these activities should only take you approximately two hours per month on average to complete. Considering there are 720 hours in a 30-day month, spending just 0.3 percent of your time each month making sure your family is protected seems a small price to pay.

Having come this far, I'm sure you don't want your plan to be rendered useless and your family left unprotected, so there's really no excuse not to make the time to regularly test and maintain your plan. Remember, it's *your* family who benefits. It's *your* choice.

22

Testing

It is a bad plan that admits of no modification.
PUBLILIUS SYRUS

Most everyone has a smoke alarm in their home. Generally, if you have a larger home you also have multiple alarms scattered throughout. Have you or your family members ever *heard* the sound these alarms make, or would the sound of the alarm – possibly waking you up in the middle of the night when the house is on fire – be unfamiliar, leaving people uncertain as to how they should respond?

Your goal is to make sure your family members survive an evacuation. They need to hear the warning signal that is designed to save their life in this situation before it goes off for real.

Let's look at how you test the emergency plan you wrote, and instill confidence in your plan and your family's ability to survive and recover.

How do I know what to test?

The good news is, not every action plan in your family emergency plan needs to be tested. Testing is only required when lack of prior knowledge may endanger people's lives.

The purpose of testing is to give each family member as much information and as many valid options as possible to survive should a disaster strike. Thinking quickly on their feet can mean the difference between life and death.

Which plans of action do I test?

The following are the plans of action which need to be tested. If you have added any customized Action Plans, you should also test the ones that impact your family's survival in a life and death situation.

- Evacuation Action Plan I (where you have time to evacuate)

- Evacuation Action Plan II (requires immediate evacuation)

- Shelter-in-Place Action Plan

- Utility Outage Action Plan

Now what?

Prior to testing your Evacuation Action Plan II (immediate evacuation), first you must have put the following in place:

- Identify two exits from each room in your home. One (generally the doorway) is considered the primary exit, and the other is your secondary escape option. Include exits for the basement, the garage, each bedroom, the kitchen, etc. Go to each room with all family members, and point out the two exits. If you need to purchase ladders or other tools to make an exit available and accessible, do so.

- Explain the exit process from both the primary and secondary exit for each room. Be sure to explain how one can exit through a window secured with bars or a door with a lock-in, lock-out deadbolt that requires a key, or a multiple-latch basement door. Teach all family members how to open all the escape routes. Place any necessary tools or keys near the relevant exit, but, don't jeopardize your security by putting these items in plain view. All family members should be aware of the location of these critical tools and keys.

- Review the location of the meeting spot outside your home. If necessary, walk outside with children to demonstrate.

- Demonstrate how to test a closed door to establish if there is fire behind it (feel it with your hand). Explain what to do when it is hot, and when it is not.

- Test the smoke alarm so all family members get to hear the sound it makes. Explain that when it sounds, each member should first try the primary exit from the room. If the primary exit is blocked by smoke and/or fire, they should immediately proceed to the secondary exit. Suggestion: Do this when you change your smoke alarm batteries in the spring and fall (daylight savings time).

- You should have a pre-determined signal to indicate that an exit route is unavailable when you are testing. You can write the word 'FIRE' on a piece of paper and fix it to a door or window to signify it is now not an available option. Observe how people react, especially children, and make sure they can easily identify their second exit.

- Determine what people should do if they are unable to use *either* exit. Suggestion: devise a family "window signal" which someone who is trapped can place in a window to notify authorities of their location. One suggestion would be to have a glow stick (you know the kind – you snap them and they glow) near each window. If you get stuck in a room, snap the stick and place it in a window. Alternatively, you could place a flashlight in each room to use as a signal. If these options do not fit into your budget, simply have some colorful paper with the word 'HELP' written on it. Bottom line: provide ways to ensure that responders can immediately pinpoint where people are trapped, so they can direct their rescue process most effectively.

Testing evacuation action plan II

Now you are ready to conduct your test. You'll remember that the goal was to exit and convene at the designated meeting spot within three minutes. If you elected to create a Personal Pack and they are kept in the house, you might want to have all members bring their Personal Pack with them during this exercise.

You need to ensure that it is a realistic test that gives all family members a chance to become familiar with the plan. Here's how to provide such a test:

- Review your Evacuation Action Plan II to make sure everyone is aware of what to do

- Recommended test frequency: twice a year

- Select one of the following scenarios to test:

    1. **Sleeping.** On a designated evening, put FIRE signs in different locations. Sound the smoke alarm, and track the time it takes family members to arrive at the designated meeting point outside your home. Check how many remembered their Personal Pack if this is part of your plan.

    2. **Evening.** When everyone is in different rooms, doing homework, watching television, talking on the telephone, etc., sound the smoke alarm and yell "TEST." Note the length of time it takes the entire family to evacuate and meet at the designated point. In this scenario, several members may not have been able to retrieve and bring their Personal Pack. Determine the impact if you want them to bring their Personal Pack as part of your plan.

    3. **Both exits blocked.** Try a test where both exists are blocked for several rooms. Determine how well your *window signal* operates in these rooms. Be sure to replenish your signals after-

wards if necessary.

4. **No adults at home.** Have your children conduct the test to see how well they respond if no adults are present. You can be there during the test, but don't participate or help them. If you have a regular babysitter or after-school guardian, you may want to conduct the test when the babysitter is at your home. Remember to also test the Communications Plan, since this scenario assumes the parents are not at home.

When you have completed the test, evaluate your family's response. Be sure to look at how pets and family members who need assistance fared. Are you confident they know what to do, and would be successful if confronted with a real disaster that required them to evacuate quickly?

If you are convinced your plan is solid, and gives the family members the best opportunity to survive, leave it unchanged and be sure to test it again in six months time. Make sure you answer any questions children might have about what they did, and remember to congratulate them on their good work.

If you are not comfortable with your family's response, you need to make adjustments. Determine what caused problems, and why, and then either change the plan or the goal (the designated meeting place) accordingly. Changes are warranted if:

- *A person on the second floor had problems unraveling their ladder to exit out the window.*

  Solution: practice unraveling the ladder, or purchase a new one if the original ladder was just too difficult or maybe too heavy.

- *Your goal required everyone to be at the designated meeting point within one minute. Be realistic when setting your timelines. If the walk from the front door to the meeting point takes a full minute, then setting a one-minute deadline prohibits successful execution of the plan.*

Solution: Change the goal so it is realistic for your situation.

- *When testing while the family was sleeping, one child did not wake up when the smoke alarm went off.*

  Solution: Add another smoke alarm near that child's bed/bedroom and/or have another family member check for this child during evacuation.

- *When testing during the evening, no one was in their bedroom so no one was able to grab their Personal Pack before exiting.*

  Solution: either have backup Personal Packs (one in the bedroom and one offsite) or determine a better location for Personal Packs (maybe the outside shed).

- *When testing during the evening, your son/daughter was in the basement playing. You had blocked the stairway up to the kitchen, meaning they had to exit through the basement hatchway. They were able to unlock the door, but were not able to push it up so they could exit.*

  Solution: Limit their play time in the basement, unless an adult is present and can provide assistance.

Testing evacuation action plan I

Evacuation Action Plan I is designed for situations where your family has prior warning, and a period of time to evacuate before danger is upon them. For this action plan, the goal is to have the car packed (kits, people and pets) and be on the road within 30 minutes.

You need to set up a few different scenarios based on what you feel is a realistic situation in your location. Points to consider for this test include:

- Review the Evacuation Action Plan I to make sure everyone is aware of what to do
- Recommended testing frequency: *twice a year*
- Select one of the following scenarios to test:

1. **Weekend morning.** Select a weekend morning and initiate the Evacuation Action Plan I by informing everyone who is present of the situation (maybe a wildfire, hurricane, flood, etc.). Identify which utilities need to be turned off. Have members perform their assigned tasks. Time the activity and see if you achieve your stated goal. If not all members are at home, use the Communications Plan to ensure that everyone knows what to do.

2. **Evening.** Follow the same procedure as in Scenario #1. Again, check if all tasks can be completed within your specified timeframe.

3. **No Adults.** As with your testing for Evacuation Action Plan II, if it's possible that your children might be at home without any adult members of the family present (with your teenagers or a babysitter in charge), conduct a test evacuation and have them drive the car to the designated shelter. Be sure they know what to do if you are not there! Have them use your Communications Plan to notify you of their progress and when they arrive at the shelter.

Once you complete the test, evaluate your family's performance. Do you feel confident they know what to do, and would be successful if confronted with a real evacuation situation? Were the any problems with pets or family members who require assistance?

Make adjustments if you feel your family was not successful. Fine-tune either the plan or the goal by determining what caused the problem and why. Some changes are warranted if:

- *Your spouse was not able to turn off the water to the house.*

  Solution: Determine what caused the failure. Was a tool needed, but unavailable? If so, get the correct tool and leave it near the water tank just in case. Maybe the person was too short, or not strong enough. If so, assign this task to a different family member.

- *Your goal was to have the car packed and moving in 10 minutes, but it took you 20 minutes.*

  Solution: Change the goal to one that is realistic for your situation, or determine if you need to pre-pack more items to make it possible to get on the road more quickly.

- *When no adults were present, the babysitter was not sure where to take your family for shelter.*

  Solution: Include regular babysitters and/or adults who supervise your children in your testing to ensure that everyone knows what to do and where to go.

Testing the shelter-in-place action plan

The Shelter-in-Place Action Plan is considered part of a life-and-death situation because you may be forced to survive for a number of days before help arrives or forced to protect your family from deadly gases or chemicals. How well prepared you are to survive this scenario might mean the difference between life and death for members of your family. You need to determine if you and your family – including any pets – can survive with the kits and plans you have put in place.

Your goal for this action plan included a timeframe you determined was appropriate for you to survive without any help from responders. Prior to Hurricane Katrina, the rule of thumb was to be prepared for three days, but as a consequence of Hurricane Katrina, many organizations are now recommending you ensure you have supplies that will enable you to survive for up to two weeks. The timeline is your choice but obviously, the longer you are able to survive, the better.

Here are some guidelines for your test:

- Review the Shelter-in-Place Action Plan to make sure everyone is aware of what to do, and where the supplies are located (remember, _you_ might not be home)
- Recommended testing frequency: twice a year
- Select one of the following scenarios to test:

   1. **Weekend.** On Friday evening, assume you are experiencing a blizzard (or a hurricane in warmer climates). Because of the heaviness of the snow and ice (and rain and wind), power lines are down over a 50-mile radius. Authorities are requesting that no one venture out unless it is an emergency. Start on Friday evening, and run into Saturday. Use only those items you have stored in your kits. Do not use any electricity. If you have electric heating, turn the heat down to 55°. You might also conduct this test over a school and/or work holiday.

   2. **No adults at home.** If your children were at home and all adult family members were at work or elsewhere, would they know what to do? Make sure the children can find the kits, prepare their own meals, understand and use the Communications Plan, stay warm if there is no heating, etc.

   3. **Chemical release.** A toxic chemical has been released in your area. You have been told by authorities to go to either the lowest or highest level in your home, and not to leave your home until you hear the _All Clear_ message. They have also recommended that if you have plastic and duct tape, you should use it to seal off openings and provide more protection from the substance that has been released. You can elect to either do this with adults involved, or test your children to see if they know what to do.

Once you complete the test, evaluate your family's performance. Are you confident they know what to do and would be successful if confronted with a real shelter-in-place scenario?

As before, if you are convinced your plan is solid and gives your family members the best opportunity to survive, you are done testing this plan.

If you do not feel your family was successful in this test, you need to make adjustments to either the plan or the goal by determining who had problems, and why. Some changes are warranted if:

- *You were testing a scenario where a chemical was released and you were told to go to the top floor but you only had the plastic pre-cut for the bathroom on the first floor.*

  Solution: Pre-cut plastic for a highest floor location and a lowest floor location.

- *You were at work, and no one at home could find the food you had stored.*

  Solution: Be sure all family members are familiar with where these kits are stored.

- *You had no entertainment activities stored, so everyone was really bored and getting cranky.*

  Solution: Add some books or board games to your kit to help keep family members entertained if they are forced to stay in the home.

Testing the utility outage action plan

For a utility outage, the goal is to be able to survive for at least four hours without supply. This includes electricity, water, and gas.

You need a realistic test that provides family members the opportunity to try out the plan when any or all of these utilities are unavailable. This is even more important if you have anyone who is particularly impacted by either cold or heat, has refrigerated medicines, needs to eat specific foods regularly, is easily dehydrated, etc.

Here are some guidelines for your test:

- Review the Utility Outage Action Plan to make sure everyone knows what to do

- Recommended testing frequency: twice a year

- Select one of the following scenarios to test:

  1. **Combine with Shelter-in-Place Action Plan test.** As part of your Shelter-in-Place test, assume either the gas, electricity, or water supply is not working.

  2. **Test one utility.** If it is water, be sure you have enough water on hand to survive for your designated period of time. If you have chosen electricity, be sure all family members can survive without this utility for a period of time without problems. This means no lights, no computers, no television, no recharging cell phones, etc. If you have elected to test the loss of your gas supply, this may impact cooking, hot water, or heating, so make sure you're prepared with alternatives.

  3. **Test beyond your goal timeframe.** If you have indicated you want to survive for up to four hours without utilities, test your plan for an eight-hour period. Make sure you are prepared.

4. **Test the worst-case season for your location.** If you feel surviving a winter without heat (or summer without air conditioning) is your worst-case scenario, test during that period. Be
   sure your worst-case scenario can be survived.

Again, once you complete the test, evaluate your family's performance.
Are you confident they know what to do, and would be successful if confronted with a real disaster?

If you are convinced your plan is solid and gives your family members
the best opportunity to survive, you are done testing this plan.

If you are not convinced your family was successful in this test, you need
to make adjustments by altering either the plan or the goal after determining
who had problems and why. Some changes are warranted if:

- *You were not at home, and your babysitter did not know what to do.*

  Solution: include the regular babysitter (or your older children, if they
  are in charge) in the test. Be sure everyone knows what to do.

- *Your goal was to survive for two hours. Your mother, who is elderly and
  has a medical condition that is made worse in extreme heat, began having
  problems after one hour.*

  Solution: You need to adjust your plan to ensure that your mother is
  immediately moved to a cool location. You may need to take them to a
  sibling's home across town, or your town may have alternative shelters
  to assist people with medical conditions. Be sure you know the maximum length of time each family member can survive when utilities are
  out.

- *You had to shut the gas off to conduct the test, and now you can't turn it
  back on.*

  Solution: Be sure everyone understands that if the gas is turned off, it
  must be restarted by the gas company. Include their number in your action plan.

At this point, your plan should be effective, and give you confidence that if your family was to experience a disaster, they now have the best possible chance of surviving and recovering from it because of your work. Don't forget to keep on testing these life-and-death scenarios regularly.

Elizabeth M. Owen

23

Maintenance

*Another flaw in the human character is that everybody
wants to build and nobody wants to do maintenance.*
KURT VONNEQUT, JR.

M aintenance. Some of us are fanatics about doing it, while others put
it off until it is, often, too late.

Think about maintenance on your car. By scheduling oil changes,
tire rotations, and regular checkups, you keep your car in good running order. The likelihood of breaking down on the side of the road is reduced. By
conducting this maintenance, you keep running costs to a minimum, get better gas mileage, and help extend the useful life of your car.

On the other hand, if you don't perform regular car maintenance tasks,
you are more likely to experience breakdowns, incur expensive repair work,
and have to replace the car sooner rather than later. Running costs rise, and
a poorly-maintained car increases the risk to your family whenever you ride
in the car.

So, why would you *not* undertake regular maintenance on your car?

There are several reasons. First, you might not have the money. When it's
time for your 30,000 mile checkup, an extra $450 may not be easy to find, so
you just skip doing the maintenance, and hope for the best. Someday soon,
when you get the extra cash, you can get the checkup done. Maybe you just

can't seem to fit it into your schedule. Changing your morning routine so you can drop the car off at the dealership and get someone to give you a ride to work can be a major juggling act, not to mention the total disruption of your whole day if you need your car for work or other things. Maybe you're just one of those people who sees a car simply as a means of getting from point A to point B. You don't maintain it, you only put gas in it when you need to go somewhere, and you only ever deal with the mechanic when it breaks down.

You've just spent valuable time writing your Emergency Plan, and so, as of this minute, your family is the proud owner of a brand new plan, and much the better for it. But, without regular maintenance, your family will quickly lose the level of protection that you have worked so hard to create. Why? Because life changes. Things happen. I promise you, your family situation will be altered, somehow, someway, by this time next year. Think about the following situations, and how they can transform your life – and your Emergency Plan:

- You get married
- You add a child to your family
- A child moves out of your home
- Your spouse dies
- You move to a new home
- Your aging parent comes to live with you
- You remodel rooms in your home
- You get a new job
- You update your Will
- You purchase new furniture for the living room
- You have a tag sale and clean out all items you no longer want

So, how do you keep your family's level of protection at its best? By performing regular maintenance on your plan, just like you do with your car. You need to set up a schedule so you regularly devote some time to making sure everything you have in your Emergency Plan is current and appropriate. Remember: disasters can happen anytime, anywhere, and to anyone. Here are some options for setting up a regular maintenance schedule:

- **Option 1** – update your plan immediately any change occurs in your circumstances. For example, if you get a new license, immediately update your plan with the new ID number, and make a backup copy. If you purchase a new bedroom set, immediately update your inventory and either take a picture or file the receipt. This is the best maintenance option, because it ensures that your Emergency Plan remains current at all times, and your family is best prepared to recover from any disaster, at any time.

- **Option 2** – update your plan on a quarterly or semi-annual basis. File all changes that are needed, then make them all at once at the scheduled time. This option is better than not maintaining your plan at all, but has the disadvantage of leaving your plan short if a disaster strikes between updates, as it almost surely will.

- **Option 3** – If you can only devote a couple of hours each month to updating your plan, you might prefer the once-a-month option. A few pages on, I have provided you with a calendar in which the tasks are spread over a 12-month period. For example, one month the tasks include reviewing and updating your plan of action for the Loss of a Spouse. It then gets reviewed at the same time each year. Option 3 is a rolling schedule, whereby you ensure that every part of your plan is updated at least once each year.

- **Option 4** – the annual update. You may decide that setting aside a specific time, once a year, works best for you. For example, Thanksgiving weekend may be the best time to update your plan, while you have the whole family gathered together. This way, everyone is involved, so everyone is on board with the changes and the latest plan. Since this should be a family activity, what better time than when everyone is together and, hopefully, in a good frame of mind. This option does leave you and your family vulnerable, in that at worst, your plan will be a full year out of date, but this sure beats not having any plan at all.

Here are some **suggestions** for your maintenance activities. Use all of them, some of them or just one of them – but make sure you do something:

- To garner the maximum benefit out of a great tax break, schedule your update of household inventory every year around November or December. Take a day one weekend and have family members clean out their own closet, then update your inventory. Take all unused items to your favorite charity. You have now cleaned out all the closets, updated your household inventory, obtained a tax break, and had the entire family participate in an exercise in giving to those less fortunate. It fits right in with the spirit of the season!

- If you're using the monthly option, set aside a specific time each month. You may decide to allocate the first Saturday of every month. On that day, you block time to complete all the tasks on that month's list. My guess is, you'll need a couple of hours, tops, each month. Isn't making your family more prepared in case disaster strikes worth that time?

Nothing says that using the 12-month calendar means you can only do a few tasks each month. You may want to fill out the calendar month-by-month, and then do all the January through March activities at one time during the first quarter of the year. Likewise, you could do the same if you only did the activities twice a year, completing the January through June activities one day during the first half of the year – whatever works for you, so long as you do it regularly.

Add Education

Remember back to the beginning of this book, when you went through a list of 46 disasters and identified those which you felt were more of a risk for you and your family? Well, now you are going to use that list.

As part of your maintenance schedule, you should take a few minutes to study one of your disaster risks. Let's say you selected tornados as a threat to your family because of where you live. Determine what your family should do if you are suddenly caught in one. How can you better safeguard your home to avoid any unnecessary damage? If you don't have a basement or lower floor to move to, what is your best bet for making yourself (and your family) safe? Update the family with any new community warning signals for tornados (if they have changed). This type of activity takes a few minutes, but may mean the difference between life and death – literally! You can approach these tasks in several ways:

- Add one or two potential disasters to your schedule of regular maintenance activities
- Select one disaster each month and review it with your family. This can even be done at the dinner table.
- Assign these tasks to your children, and have them present the information to the family
- After researching, put the information in a three-ring notebook for future reference, and as a guide for next year's update

For each disaster you review, educate yourself and your family on the following:

- Community warnings for the disaster, if any
- How much time you have to reach safety once you hear or see the signal
- What *getting to safety* means (give examples of where to go)

- How you know when the event is over and it is safe to emerge
- How long after the event it might be before you see the first responders in the area
- What you can do before the event to minimize damage (check to see if your community has any *disaster resistant* recommendations, which may also be called hazard mitigation programs)
- The time(s) of the year this type of disaster normally occurs
- What radio station to tune in to for the most current information
- When it would be safe to attempt to use your Communication Plan, and what to do if it does not work
- Conduct what many organizations call a *home hazard hunt* to remove any items which might cause more damage to your home or family from that type of disaster

Maintenance Calendars

The following calendars are provided for you to evenly spread out maintenance activities related to your family emergency plan.

There are only two months which are 100% set for you. They are generically identified as SPRING and FALL. These correspond to the two months when we change our clocks to accommodate Daylight Saving Time. In 2007, these months changed are March and November but Congress may swap them back to April and October should the findings of their study determine the change resulted in no energy savings.

Maintenance Calendar for SPRING

☐ Test Evacuation Action Plan II
☐ Test Shelter-in-Place Action Plan
☐ Change batteries in smoke alarm(s)
☐ Change batteries in carbon monoxide alarm(s)
☐ Have air conditioning/heating system checked/cleaned
☐ Review Emergency Plan member list and cover page
☐ Review and update Clothing and Bedding Kit (season appropriate)
☐ Refresh water in Water Kit, if needed
☐ Refresh food in Food Kit, if needed
☐ Check spare tire(s)
☐ _____
☐ _____

Maintenance Calendar for FALL

☐ Test Evacuation Action Plan II
☐ Test Utility Outage Action Plan
☐ Change batteries in smoke alarm(s)
☐ Change batteries in carbon monoxide alarm(s)
☐ Have air conditioning/heating system checked/cleaned
☐ Review 'List of 46" and make adjustments, if applicable
☐ Review and update Clothing and Bedding Kit (season appropriate)
☐ Refresh water in Water Kit, if needed
☐ Refresh food in Food Kit, if needed
☐ Check spare tire(s)
☐ _____
☐ _____

Maintenance Calendar for _____

- ☐ Review and update Communication Plan
- ☐ Review and update Loss of Home Action Plan
- ☐ Review and talk about one disaster risk: _____
- ☐ Take a CPR class (or other first aid training)
- ☐ Update, renew, and test home security system, if applicable
- ☐ _____
- ☐ _____
- ☐ _____
- ☐ _____

Maintenance Calendar for _____

- ☐ Review and update Loss of Adult Member Action Plan(s)
- ☐ Review and update Loss of Child Member Action Plan(s)
- ☐ Review and talk about one disaster risk: _____
- ☐ Review and update Critical Records Kit(s)
- ☐ _____
- ☐ _____
- ☐ _____
- ☐ _____

Maintenance Calendar for _____

- ☐ Review and update Personal Record Kit(s)
- ☐ Add complete record for new member(s)
- ☐ Review and update Personal Pack(s)
- ☐ Review and talk about one disaster risk: _____
- ☐ _____
- ☐ _____
- ☐ _____
- ☐ _____

Maintenance Calendar for _____

- ☐ Test Evacuation Action Plan I
- ☐ Review and talk about one disaster risk: _____
- ☐ Review and update inventory for electronics
- ☐ Review and update inventory for living room (include storage/closets)
- ☐ _____
- ☐ _____
- ☐ _____
- ☐ _____

Elizabeth M. Owen

Maintenance Calendar for _____

- ☐ Review and update Identity Theft Action Plan
- ☐ Review and update Loss of Critical Documents Action Plan
- ☐ Review and talk about one disaster risk: _____
- ☐ Review and update inventory for dining room (include storage/closets)
- ☐ _____
- ☐ _____
- ☐ _____
- ☐ _____

Maintenance Calendar for _____

- ☐ Review and update Member Goodbye Records
- ☐ Review and talk about one disaster risk: _____
- ☐ Review and update inventory for the garage
- ☐ Review and update inventory for the storage unit
- ☐ Review and update inventory for tools
- ☐ Check spare tire(s)
- ☐ _____
- ☐ _____
- ☐ _____
- ☐ _____

Maintenance Calendar for _____

- ☐ Review and update Loss of Household Goods Action Plan
- ☐ Review Loss of Job/Income Action Plan
- ☐ Review and talk about one disaster risk: _____
- ☐ Review and update inventory for basement
- ☐ Review and update inventory for collectibles
- ☐ _____
- ☐ _____
- ☐ _____
- ☐ _____

Maintenance Calendar for _____

- ☐ Review and update Loss of Transportation Action Plan
- ☐ Review and Update Loss of Pet Action Plan
- ☐ Review and talk about one disaster risk: _____
- ☐ Review and update inventory for outdoor/landscape
- ☐ _____
- ☐ _____
- ☐ _____
- ☐ _____

Maintenance Calendar for _____

- ☐ Review and update inventory for kitchen (include storage / pantry / closets)
- ☐ Review and update inventory for safe deposit box
- ☐ Review and update inventory for attic
- ☐ Review and talk about one disaster risk: _____
- ☐ _____
- ☐ _____
- ☐ _____
- ☐ _____

Maintenance Calendar for _____

- ☐ Review and update First Aid Kit
- ☐ Review and update Tools and Supplies Kit
- ☐ Review and update inventory for home office/den
- ☐ Review and update software inventory (all computers)
- ☐ Review and talk about one disaster risk: _____
- ☐ _____
- ☐ _____
- ☐ _____
- ☐ _____

Conclusion

Well done! You should be very proud of yourself. You have now completed an Emergency Plan that greatly increases your chances of surviving and recovering from any loss that may come your way. My hope is that you never have to use it, but if you do, you are now prepared and ready to face anything that is thrown at you, no matter how unlikely. Because, actually, it can happen to you!

Elizabeth M. Owen

24

Distribution

Wisdom is knowing what to do next,
skill is knowing how to do it,
and virtue is doing it.
DAVID STARR JORDAN

O nce you have your plan written, you should have copies made. Consider providing copies to your other family members who do not live with you. Or, possibly and/or in addition to family copies, leave a copy at work (in a locked drawer). You can also put a copy inside your Clothing and Bedding Kit or Personal Pack so it goes with you if you evacuate. Your attorney may also be an option so long as all family members know where it is located and can get at it should it be needed. Don't forget about putting a copy in your safe deposit box being sure at least one other family member has access. And, your remote contact is also a logical choice for keeping a copy.

If you live alone or away from where your family lives, be sure to get copies to your backup person or at least let them know where this information is kept. They will be the one(s) around to help your family should something happen to you. What a help this will be for your family.

Author's biography

ELIZABETH OWEN has been the owner of Fundamental Writes (www.fundamentalwrites.com) since 2001. She has held jobs in records management, corporate disaster planning, as a bookkeeper, systems analyst, technical writer, product planner, usability lab manager, a member of a PMO, product marketing manager, and classroom instructor/faculty (corporate and college). These jobs have crisscrossed industries including banking, pharmaceuticals, travel, accounting firms, beef processing plants, art museums, and a software company. She holds a Bachelor of Science in Technical Management from Regis University in Denver, CO and a Master of Science in Technical and Professional Communication from Southern Polytechnic State University in Marietta, GA. She is a volunteer member of the Wallingford (Connecticut) Health Department Emergency Planning team. Elizabeth is a dual citizen of the US and Ireland and enjoys writing, speaking, being a part-time faculty member, and traveling the world.

Comments and suggestions

If you would like to send me any comments or suggestions on how you have used this process, you can write to me at info@fundamentalwrites.com. Check this website to see the best comments published. Each person will receive credit for their contributions.

For all of you who used this process to create a family emergency plan, test it regularly, and maintain it year-over-year, I hope YOUR LIFE never gets interrupted.

Index